D1444133

THE REFERRAL PROCESS IN LIBRARIES:

a characterization and an exploration of related factors

by

George S. Hawley

The Scarecrow Press, Inc.
Metuchen, N.J., & London
1987

Library of Congress Cataloging-in-Publication Data

Hawley, George S., 1944–
    The referral process in libraries.

    Includes indexes.
    Bibliography: p.
    1. Referral centers (Information services)
2. Reference services (Libraries) I. Title.
Z674.4.H38 1987 025.5'2774   87–9201
ISBN 0–8108–2010–2

CONTENTS

5 SUMMARY AND CONCLUSIONS

PREFACE

This study sought to identify factors that influence library referral, and many such factors were identified. In this sense it is a diffuse presentation, confronting the reader with the challenge of following many separate concepts.

It is also largely about a single concept: equity. Equity, however, was recognized as the central theme only after the interview data were analyzed, so the subject of equity is introduced gradually, beginning in the third chapter. Furthermore, when a definition of equity is provided early in the "Results" chapter, it is noted that the term can have more than one meaning even in the field of social psychology, and a further expansion of meanings is made in the following two chapters. Admittedly this does not make the equity theme as easy to follow as it would have been if it had been selected from the start as the subject of the research, or if only a single conception of equity were being considered.

The meaning of the concept of library referral also evolves, being provided in the first chapter with a broad, "working" definition; then narrowed into a functional definition fitting the study's findings in the "Results" chapter; and finally provided with a more complete definition in the final chapter.

Appreciation for their valuable advice during the course of this study is due the members of the dissertation committee:

Mr. Hendrik Edelman, Dr. Herbert R. Kells, and Dr. Donald R. King of the School of Communication, Information and Library Studies, Rutgers University, and Dr. David Carr of the Graduate School of Education, Rutgers University. Dr. Kells' intelligence, thoroughness, and responsiveness made him an ideal chairperson and principal advisor.

Thanks are also due to the library directors who agreed to let their institutions participate and to the librarians who spoke at length and with considerable candor.

George S. Hawley
Newark Public Library
Newark, N.J.

CHAPTER 1

BACKGROUND AND RATIONALE

THE MOTIVATION OF LIBRARY REFERRAL

Introspective reference librarians might have a number of concerns regarding referral of users to other institutions, such as their own library's policies regarding referrals, the inconvenience to the user in being sent elsewhere, and the reaction of staff in the location to which the user is sent. Other librarians, perhaps in the same library, may rarely think of referring, feeling that their responsibility to the user ends once they have indicated what their own library has on a topic.

Why are some referrals made and not others? Library literature provides surprisingly few answers, but some direction is to be found in McClure and Hernon's 1983 study of reference service at selected U.S. Government Printing Office depositories in academic libraries. The authors asked "what factors can be identified that encourage or discourage the referral of the reference question to another person on the library staff or information provider and how can the effectiveness of the referral process related to government publications be described?" (p. 16).

Their findings indicated that willingness to refer did not show a statistically significant relationship with the eight

1

institutional variables studied: highest degree offered; library volumes and budgets; percentage of depository item
numbers selected; collection organization; and total librarians,
document librarians, and paraprofessionals on the staff (p.
97). Regarding reference activities in general, it was learned
that "the most important criterion related to answering questions correctly is the competency of individual documents staff
members, their interest in public service and their personal
ability to negotiate a variety of reference questions and to
engage in problem solving" (p. 86).

McClure and Hernon mention six studies of reference
service which point to the conclusion that "general reference
staffs infrequently engage in referral activity either within or
outside the institution" (p. 89). Their own study discovered
that documents personnel "tend to view their collections as
self-contained; if they perceive that they lack the immediate
resources to address an information need, they seldom call
upon co-workers or other information providers--even regional depositories to which, in theory, they report" (p. 104).
The research technique used by McClure and Hernon was
"unobtrusive," meaning that staff members did not know that
they were being examined. Responses by the staff members
who were studied to the preselected questions showed an
overall accuracy rate of only 37 percent, below the average
of approximately 50 percent found in other unobtrusive tests.

McClure and Hernon note that the literature of librarianship most frequently examines referral activity within the
context of information and referral services (I&R), usually
operated out of public libraries. They state:

> An important aspect of I&R is to research more seg-
> ments of the general population and to assist them
> in meeting a wider variety of their information needs.
> I&R centers within the libraries supplement informa-
> tion in printed reference sources and provide cur-
> rent information on the community, perhaps through
> the maintenance of community information files.
> [p. 89]

Childers (1979) defines I&R as "facilitating the link
between a person with a need and the service, activity, information, or advice outside the library which can meet the
need" (p. 2036). He too finds that it "ordinarily involves

the development and maintenance of a resource file--a current list of resources and information about them" (p. 2936). He explains:

> The biggest barrier to finding out anything about
> I&R is settling on a definition of it. To some librar-
> ians, I&R is unique in a library setting and in no
> way resembles standard activities and services in
> libraries. To others, it is nothing more than a minor
> variation on the theme of traditional reference serv-
> ice. [p. 2936]

Elsewhere, Childers (1980, p. 928) makes a distinction between "steering"--simply providing directions to another resource-- and "referring"--actually trying to make the contact for the client.

McClure and Hernon observe that library literature also examines referral activity in the context of cooperative refer- ence service and networking. Statewide or local networks permit individual libraries to transmit reference questions that they are not able to answer throughout a hierarchical network (p. 89). A formidable list of barriers that hamper the development of such formal channels has been provided by Nolting (1969): fear of loss of local autonomy, fear of loss of availability of library materials due to use by others, local bias, lack of funding, disagreement over the role of the larger library versus smaller libraries, distance, legal and administrative restrictions, and lack of information and ex- perience.

Childers (1980, p. 926) performed an unobtrusive study of reference service among the public libraries belonging to the Suffolk (N.Y.) Cooperative Library System, using the "new departure" of testing the response of the sources to which referrals were made. Two-thirds of the out-of-library resources were either correct or mostly correct. The others consisted mostly of further steering.

A WORKING DEFINITION OF REFERRAL

Some ambiguity exists in the currently available defini- tions of library referral. McClure and Hernon begin their chapter on referral by documents librarians with Childers'

above-mentioned definition of the more specialized I&R:
"facilitating the link between a person with a need and the
service, activity, information, or advice outside the library
which can meet the need." They then state that "referral
also encompasses sending a patron to another library staff
member or department. It can therefore occur within and
outside a particular library setting" (p. 87). Next, they
seem to include interlibrary loan in their definition of referral:

> The depository library program, in theory, encour-
> ages referral so that depository libraries will attempt
> to meet the information needs of their own clientele
> while also extending backup assistance to other de-
> pository libraries. This assistance might be in the
> form of interlibrary loans or answers to specific
> questions. [p. 87]

Finally, they use the term in the broadest sense, to include
directing someone to a reference tool (as well as to another
library employee): "Referral, as is evident, can be more
than sending someone to the card catalog, a particular reference source, or member of the library staff" (p. 89).

There is a problem in starting with a definition of
I&R when defining library referral in general. I&R concen-
trates on linking users to specialist agencies serving the
same geographic area (thus the emphasis on community information files). In many referral situations, however, librarians depend on assistance from other libraries whose
primary responsibility is to serve other geographic communities or restricted clienteles. Often the librarian will obtain
the information or material for the user because a lengthy
interview or interaction between the resource called upon and
the user is not required (as it likely would be in dealing
with a social service agency), and either because it is easier
for the user or protocols have been established to assure
that libraries are not burdened unnecessarily with outside
users. Thus in the New Jersey Library Network when a
librarian transmits a reference question to the next level in
the hierarchy it is called a "reference referral." Therefore
it seemed possible that the definition of referral should include both the concept of the librarian helping the user to
make direct contact with an outside source of information,
and the concept of the librarian making the entire contact

for the user. Interlibrary loan, free exchange of photocopies, and the forwarding of reference questions, then,
received tentative inclusion.

Is it also correct to describe directing someone to the
card catalog or to a reference source as an act of referral?
Probably not. One certainly might say, "I referred him to
the card catalog," but one is unlikely to say, "I made a referral to the card catalog." A referral involving service
to a client or user implies exposing the person to someone
else's realm of direct responsibility. The user or his or her
query is directed to another location where another individual
is in control. If an art reference librarian points to an art
encyclopedia and says, "Look there," it is an act of referring to an encyclopedia. It may even be an act of referral,
in some sense of the word. However, in terms of practical
delimitation of meaning, it is not considered here to be library referral, and was not considered to be in the working
use of the term in collecting data for this dissertation.
Initially the topic of library referral was interpreted broadly, so as to possibly include interlibrary loan and obtaining
an answer to a question from another institution for a user,
but the act of directing a user to an inanimate reference
source, not under the direct supervision of another library
staff member, was considered to be an act of reference, not
referral.

FINDINGS FROM OTHER SETTINGS

Outside of McClure and Hernon's findings mentioned
above regarding the lack of influence on referral of several
institutional variables, the library literature offers little
careful analysis of what causes an individual librarian to
make a referral. An indication of the broad range of possible influencing factors can be found outside library literature, however.

These studies have pointed to such factors as: group
identity among teachers (Brady, 1972), numbers of years in
practice by family physicians (Brock, 1977), policemen's
friendships with employees of outside agencies (Johnson,
1971), convenience of family physicians (Metcalfe & Sischy,
1974), and personal acquaintanceship of clergy with mental
health professionals (Hong & Wiehe, 1974; Lee, 1976).

Elkins' (1983) dissertation found that, while educational level accounted for 9.4 percent of ministers' referrals to psychological counseling, the other variables tested--age, counseling training, number of mental-health-related individuals and agencies available in the community, self-esteem level, counseling role perception, years in the ministry, size of community, theological orientation, and size of congregation--collectively account for less than 7 percent.

At the same time, writers have remarked on a dearth of material relating to the topic. Metcalfe and Sischy, writing in 1973, found virtually no studies of family physician referral in the United States. In 1976 Lee wrote that the few texts in the therapeutic disciplines that mentioned referral at all gave the subject a cursory discussion. Paritzky, in 1981, noted that a review of the literature on counseling uncovered a paucity of written material on the referral task. In 1979 Scott, Dean, Johnston, and Nussbaum reported that much of police referral literature was program descriptive and complained that "theories of police referral are nonexistent" (p. 135).

In literature not relating to librarianship, referral is usually left undefined. In January 1984, a definition was sought across all BRS (Bibliographic Retrieval Service, Inc.) computerized data bases using the company's "CROSS" searching technique. This produced a definition in the health literature of "successful referral" as "one in which the patient made contact with a treatment facility of the indicated problem, and information concerning evaluation and management of the referred patient was transmitted to the referring facility" (Dickinson, Novick & Asnes, 1976, p. 138). Using this criterion, a librarian could give a user accurate information on how to contact an agency, but if the user did not make the contact, or if the place referred to did not inform the referring library what treatment was provided, the referral would be called unsuccessful.

PROBLEM STATEMENT

Although library users need referral since no one library can satisfy all requests on its own, studies indicate that librarians often will neither answer a question correctly nor furnish a referral. Since relatively little is known about the factors that may cause or inhibit referral, a basic, exploratory study seemed necessary to pursue these matters.

CHAPTER 2

RESEARCH PLAN

PURPOSE OF STUDY

Since library referral was a relatively unexplored topic, this study was descriptive in nature and qualitative. It searched for qualities amid descriptive data rather than precisely measuring or quantifying preselected qualities. Several purposes were stated for research.

Due to the need for further attention to definition and taxonomy, the first purpose was to identify and define the types of referral engaged in by librarians. Secondly, the study sought to examine the factors that seem to influence librarians' decisions to refer inquiries. The variability and complexity of the factors were shown through detailed descriptions of librarians' accounts of their attitudes and behavior.

Thirdly, an attempt was made to explore the extent of influence of the various factors. It was recognized that some may affect only a few librarians, but very strongly; others may affect most librarians moderately, and so on.

The fourth purpose was to explore the interaction of the factors. The intention was to take the static model of the referral process, built around referring librarians, their

8

coworkers and supervisors, the users, and the outsiders to whom referrals are made, and to develop it further towards an interactive, systems-like model, in which the presence of one factor is seen to influence the existence of others.*

Next, realizing that the question of "good" referral is to some extent a question of individual values, various conceptions of "good" referral were explored along with the factors that seem to influence the formation of these different conceptions and facilitate their realization.

Finally, as theory building progressed and the first attempt to set forth a systems model of the library referral process was made, connections were drawn to relevant existing theories.

Several specific research questions can be stated as follows: How should referral by librarians be defined? What factors influence the decision to make a referral or the way in which the referral is made? Which appear to be the major factor or factors? How do the various factors interrelate? What seem to be the attributes of "good" library referral? In what ways can good referral be achieved? How do the findings, or resultant theory, relate to findings and theories of other researchers?

GENERAL METHODOLOGICAL PRINCIPLES

The research idea was based on the author's personal experience as a reference librarian, most recently with statewide responsibility for reference and referral as head of New Jersey's regional U.S. documents depository, located at Newark Public Library, and on literature directly or

*Gellner (1964) describes a model as "the indication of a simpler more accurately determinable state of affairs, with the intention of facilitating deduction of further consequences which can then be tentatively reapplied to the more complex and elusive real system. By describing a system by means of definite postulates which specify the properties of the model, and thus in a way give rise to it, it becomes possible to deduce further consequences from the postulates and about the model by rigorous deduction" (p. 435).

indirectly relating to referral. "A valuable part of the data
for behavioral science is provided by self-observation,"
states Kaplan (1964), who observes: "It is by way of observation that introspective materials assume particular importance: the village idiot finds the strayed horse by asking himself where he would go if he were a horse--and there
it is!" (p. 142). In The Discovery of Grounded Theory,
Glaser and Strauss (1967) write that

> one should deliberately cultivate such reflections on
> personal experience. Generally we suppress them,
> or give them the status of mere opinions (for ex-
> ample, opinions about what is true of fraternities,
> having belonged to one before becoming a sociolo-
> gist), rather than looking at them as springboards
> to systematic theorizing. [p. 252]

A literature review preliminary to the conduct of such
a qualitative study is helpful in justifying and clarifying the
research topic. The extent, however, to which it should
guide the research is disputed. Glaser and Strauss challenge the belief that

> formal theories can be applied directly to a substan-
> tive area, and will supply most or all of the neces-
> sary concepts and hypotheses. The consequence is
> often a forcing of data, as well as a neglect of rele-
> vant concepts and hypotheses that may emerge.
> [p. 34]

They claim that

> an effective strategy is, at first, literally to ignore
> the literature of theory and fact on the area under
> study, in order to assure that the emergence of
> categories will not be contaminated by concepts more
> suited to different areas. Similarities and conver-
> gences with the literature can be established after
> the analytic core of categories has emerged. [p. 37]

Later, they concede, however, that some researchers read
"extensively" before beginning field work, adding: "There
is no ready formula, of course: one can only experiment to
find which gives the best results" (p. 253).

For the present research, studies specifically relating to the causes of referral, along with a number of topics which were thought possibly to relate to referral were examined in a broad, "initial" literature review. The topics can be identified as follows: goals, autonomy in decision making, peer pressure, training, personality, embarrassment, ethics, institutional cooperation, outside personal contacts, and cost to the client. The review gave some guidance in the formation of questions asked of librarians in interviews. It was not meant to provide support for specific hypotheses as would be true in a study emphasizing the precise testing of carefully formulated hypotheses or other statements. It was meant, rather, to create a broad, sensitizing atmosphere in which the researcher could be alert to any significant input from the librarians interviewed. The part of the review that was found to be relevant to the results of this study are presented in Appendix A.

Once factors thought to influence the referral process were uncovered through empirical, qualitative analysis, a second literature review was undertaken in order to relate them more directly to the literature. That review appears in Chapter 4.

Since the present research sought a theory of the referral process rather than the verification of an existing one, Glaser and Strauss's ideas on theory generation were of interest. The elements of theory that they suggest should be generated through a technique of comparative analysis are "first, conceptual categories and their conceptual properties; and second, hypotheses or generalized relations among the categories and their properties" (p. 35). They observe that "when the main emphasis is on verifying theory, there is no provision for discovering novelty, and potentially illuminating perspectives, that do emerge and might change the theory, actually are suppressed" (p. 40).

Their "constant comparative method" calls for the analyst to code "each incident in his data into as many categories as possible, as categories emerge or as data emerge that fit an existing category" (p. 105). Citing an example from their own research for their book, Awareness of Dying, Glaser and Strauss state that the category of "social loss" of dying patients emerged quickly from nurses' responses to

the potential deaths of their patients. The constant comparison of incidents

> very soon starts to generate theoretical properties
> of the category. The analyst starts to think in
> terms of the full range of types or continua of the
> category, its dimensions, the conditions under which
> it is pronounced or minimized, its major conse-
> quences, its relation to other categories, and its
> other properties. For example, while constantly
> comparing incidents on how nurses respond to the
> social loss of dying patients, we realized that some
> patients are perceived as a high social loss and
> others as a low social loss, and that patient care
> tends to vary positively with degree of social loss.
> [p. 106]

Similarly, in proposing to investigate librarians' in-
clinations to refer, it seemed possible to achieve some explanations by using qualitative methods. In fact, it was
realized that reference librarians might judge the social
worth of their clients in much the same way that nurses
judge the social worth of their dying patients, but it was
not known how many relevant factors would not display such
obvious causal links, or even clear associations. The notion
of "goals" for instance could have been as important to referral as the type of client, but could have proven much
more difficult to decipher.

In his follow-up book, Theoretical Sensitivity: Advances in the Methodology of Grounded Theory (1978), Glaser
elaborates on another aspect of his and Strauss's approach
that might have had only limited applicability:

> The analyst should consciously look for a core vari-
> able when coding his data. As he constantly com-
> pares incidents and concepts he will generate many
> codes, while being alert to the one or two that are
> core. He is constantly looking for the "main
> theme." [p. 94]

Later Glaser states that

> typically sociological monographs are constructed on
> the basis of a "little logic".... The little logic

usually consists of no more than a pargraph or two,
and often just one long sentence. [p. 129]

He asserts that the little logic can provide the core variable
that explains a large amount of the variation in a behavior
or set of behaviors, as in his and Strauss's conclusion in
Awareness of Dying that awareness contexts account for
much of the behavior around a dying patient in a hospital
(p. 129). Furthermore, a single little logic is all that is
needed in grounded theory: "Books without any wander
all over and books with two ... find difficulty in handling
both together adequately" (p. 130). Glaser thus favors the
discovery of a single vital theory. So many factors can influence referral behavior, however, that a single one of
overriding importance might not have been distinguished.

    Glaser also notes that the little logic "implies whether
the study will be descriptive, verificational or focus on theory generation" (p. 129). This dissertation is not verificational. It aimed ultimately at theory generation, but it in-
tends also to be descriptive. With so many possible factors
influencing referral, merely describing them will be useful.
As George W. Brown (1973) says, "Things are described
which appear to go together, and in doing so, some sense
is made of the world" (p. 2). He cites as an example Cuber
and Harroff's (1965) evocative classification of marriages into
the five types of conflict habituated, devitalized, passive
congenial, vital, or total (p. 2).

    This study was in general in the spirit of Glaser and
Strauss, but with a dollop of the humility expressed by Lee
J. Cronbach (1975), who in his Distinguished Scientific Contribution Award address to the American Psychological Association protested that "the explanations we live by will
perhaps always remain partial, and distant from real events"
(p. 123). "We need to reflect on what it means to establish
empirical generalizations in a world in which most effects
are interactive," Cronbach warned (p. 121). Basically in
sympathy with Glaser and Strauss, he contended:

    The two scientific disciplines, experimental control
    and systematic correlation, answer formal questions
    stated in advance. Intensive local observation goes
    beyond discipline to an open-eyed, open-minded ap-
    preciation of the surprises nature deposits in the
    investigative net. [p. 125]

SPECIFIC METHODOLOGY

Regarding specific techniques of the current study, the following passage from The Discovery of Grounded Theory is significant:

> ...data collected according to a preplanned routine are more likely to force the analyst into irrelevant directions and harmful pitfalls. He may discover unanticipated contingencies in his respondents, in the library and in the field, but is unable to adjust his collection procedures or even redesign his whole project. [p. 48]

Later Glaser and Strauss claim that "the sociologist who wishes to generate theory cannot state beforehand how many groups he will study and to what degree he will study each one." He can, however, specify the kinds of groups, which will "indicate the range of types necessary to achieve the desired scope and conceptual generality and to maximize differences for developing properties" (p. 74).

If this study were an attempt at verification, attention likely would have been given to sample size needed to achieve statistical significance. A mailed questionnaire containing carefully pretested questions, requiring answers with little or no variation in wording, would likely have been employed. Since this was an exploratory study, it was not certain in advance what amount of data would be required to obtain meaningful results. The data gathering technique chosen was in-person interviewing, with questions that were "open-ended" (interviewees used their own wording) and, to the extent possible, "non-directive" (interviewees determined topics of discussion). Interviews were scheduled until the researcher felt no major concepts were being discovered.

The initial intention was to interview in academic, public and special libraries. Such a broad approach was supported by Glaser and Strauss's Awareness of Dying, for which extremes in types of hospitals and wards were studied in order to accumulate a vast number of diverse, qualitative "facts," even if some facts were slightly inaccurate (p. 266). However, it was decided not to interview at special libraries since in general the size of their professional staffs were

too small to permit three or four interviews per institution.
It was also decided not to formally interview at any libraries
housing a million or more volumes. Some insight into these
large libraries was gained by asking those who were interviewed who had worked at such places to explain those settings.

A letter accompanied by a reply postcard (see Appendix B) was sent to library directors inviting their libraries' participation in the project. Ten letters were mailed
in April 1983, one in May, and five in June. One director
declined to participate via the postcard. Two directors (including the only director of a special library contacted)
telephoned to decline, citing a lack of referral activity.
Telephone calls were made to the three directors who did
not reply. One explained that his staff had refused to
participate. At a second library the director's secretary
said that the staff did not have time to be interviewed,
and at the third library the director's secretary also said
that a shortage of staff would prevent participation. In
one of the ten libraries that did participate, two of the four
librarians present on the day that interviews were being conducted declined to be interviewed.

Description of the libraries studied is restricted by
the need for confidentiality. The letter asking library directors to participate stated that, while "each interview will
last about an hour and will be tape recorded," the "identities of the libraries and of the librarians will not be disclosed."

If this were a study of a number of similar libraries,
or if information collected pertained to matters that are difficult to link with particular individuals or libraries, there
would be less need for concern over concealing identities.
Instead, only from one to three libraries in each of the five
categories of small, medium, and large sized public libraries;
and small and medium sized academic libraries; were selected
for in-depth, tape-recorded interviewing of several librarians. A total of five academic and five public libraries were
chosen. Most of these interviews provided over an hour of
detailed information regarding practices and attitudes.

Besides the need to safeguard confidentiality, another
reason not to present data on collection size, number of

staff, budget, subject strengths, network membership, interlibrary loan statistics, and other information on the libraries visited is that this type of detail did not seem to
lead to interesting hypotheses or relationships concerning
the referral process. Much of these data were collected by
reading directories, library history files, and descriptive
pamphlets; and by asking questions (statistics on referral
of users were sought but not found in any of the libraries
studied). Certainly being a member of a network increased
the likelihood of referring through that network, and being
a U.S. documents depository increased the likelihood of receiving referrals for documents but, at least in the absence
of statistics indicating an unusual pattern, the conclusions
concerning these matters are not very profound. The chapter on the results contains some general descriptive information.

   Following what has been said about confidentiality,
there seems to be no compelling reason to identify the state
or states involved. All libraries were reached by public
transportation from the writer's former home in New Bruns-
wick, NJ, and neither time nor funding allowed for very
distant travel. It should be noted that, besides looking for
a variety in types of libraries, there was some attempt to
choose several libraries in close proximity to one another,
allowing for the study of more intense patterns of interaction.

   There is another reason not to try to identify a state
or states. In the ten libraries, 34 librarians (22 female and
12 male) were interviewed and tape recorded about their
present libraries. Fourteen librarians briefly described previous positions at a total of fifteen libraries in other states,
so the data reflect this out-of-state dimension as well.

   The issue of location information is a further complicated one. One librarian had only been in her present
position a couple of weeks, and so was interviewed at length
about her previous reference position in another library.
Of all the librarians recorded, seven described positions in
a total of nine other libraries in the same state as their current positions. Another nineteen librarians were interviewed
informally in various places: at lunch, in an automobile,
waiting for the start of a meeting, and so on. A teacher was
asked about inter-community and intra-community hostility.

Two students were asked about their use of libraries. To
broaden the perspective even further, a medical doctor and
a supervisor of a crisis "hotline" were asked questions about
their referral practices.

It was thought to be unwise to conduct interviews
without a prepared list of questions, even though the intention was to have the librarians express themselves as
spontaneously as possible about the major determinants of
their referrals. This proved to be a good choice. Opening
questions asking librarians to describe a recent referral,
and to state the effect that "other libraries, your own library, and the user, yourself, and your fellow librarians"
had on their referral brought little response. Interviews
were similar to those described by William Foote Whyte
(1982) in a study of human relations in restaurants:

> I began each interview simply by asking the infor-
> mant to tell me the job situation. The usual answer
> was: "What do you want to know?" Some informants
> were willing to respond to questions, but no one
> poured out his feelings in response to my general
> invitation. Rather, the approach seemed to make
> the informants quite uneasy, and I quickly shifted
> to providing a good deal more structure in the in-
> terview. [p. 111]

The interviews were, therefore, "structured": there
was a list of questions to be covered. Refinements were
made as experience was gained, but in general the following
questions were covered:

1. "Tell me about any referrals made today or recently, or tell me about your referrals in general." This question could lead to an involved answer, as when the intrica-
cies of interlibrary loan procedure were described on the
supposition that it was a variant of referral. Previous em-
ployment was covered to an extent also.

2. "How do you define referral?" This question was
usually asked during the response to the first question.
Regardless of how narrowly the librarian defined referral,
it was explained that for the purpose of the interview the
subject would be interpreted broadly, to include in-building
and out-of-building referral, and both suggesting the user

make contact with another source and the library obtaining the information or material.

3. "What effect have other libraries, your own library, the user, yourself, and your fellow librarians had on your referral?" Generally, this question proved to be too abstract to elicit much response.

4. "Is referral encouraged in your library (as by a written policy statement, forms for recording referral, or card files or other referral aids)?"

5. "How much freedom do you have in deciding how you will perform reference and referral?"

6. "What influence does the behavior of your coworkers have?" "Coworkers" meant people working in the same library.

7. "How important are friendly relations with outside contacts?"

8. "How much consideration do you give to the physical, monetary, and mental cost to the client?"

9. "Do you receive feedback?"

10. "What influence does the attractiveness and personality of the user have?"

11. "What service is owed to outsiders?"

12. "Does the referral process ever cause you embarrassment?"

13. "Does overenthusiasm or tiredness affect your referral?"

14a. "How would you define good and bad referral, and what are the causes of each?" This question was asked in the first four libraries, but its abstractness and similarity to a school essay question caused librarians some discomfort and stifled their responses to an extent. Subsequently, the next question was asked instead.

14b. "A number of studies, most recently McClure and Hernon's, have indicated generally poor quality reference and referral work. What do you think are the causes of this problem?"

A general principle followed was to go from more general questions to more specific, so as not to influence the responses unnecessarily. Another was to save the more personal questions until the end, after the interviewee felt more at ease. However, so as not to interrupt the natural flow of conversation, the questions were not always covered in the sequence presented here.

Two pretest interviews were taped in December 1982. At the ten participating libraries, interviews were conducted as follows: three libraries in May 1983, two in June, three in July, and two in August. This schedule allowed time to transcribe interviews and to consider modifications of questions between libraries.

Reading the transcripts did not immediately reveal the broad conclusions eventually arrived at. To sort the data by topic, and to compare and contrast concepts, significant statements from the handwritten transcripts were transferred to about fourteen hundred typed index cards. During the typing each card was coded with one of 15 preliminary subject codes, and codes for the name of the library, the name of the librarian, and the transcript page number. The cards were then sorted into about 26 categories, including 6 abstract categories, such as "independence," and 20 more situation-specific categories, such as "personal contacts of the librarian," "interlibrary loan," and "feedback." In addition, there were about 47 subcategories, such as "promoting interlibrary loan" and "organized feedback." To assist in generalizing the data, each card was then summarized in a line or two, and each of these one- or two-line concepts was coded with one or more of the six abstract qualities. It was discovered that nearly all could be fitted in either the abstract quality of efficiency or equity. Eventually through combination and elimination the 20 situation-specific categories were reduced to 14 factors relating to the librarian's own library, outside resources, and the user.

LIMITATIONS

1.   The specific methodology chosen places some limitations on the objective of discovering factors influencing referral.   Ideally, there would have been long hours of ob-
serving the behavior of librarians, in addition to the interviewing, just as Glaser and Strauss not only interviewed in
hospitals but also observed interpersonal behavior.   Of
course, observation in libraries may not have revealed as
general and intriguing a phenomenon as the varying degree
to which people make obvious their awareness of imminent
death.

2.   While an attempt was made not to appear judgmental (buttressed by genuine indecision regarding how to define "good" referral once everyone's interests are taken into
consideration), some librarians probably deliberately con-
cealed some dimensions about their library or their own behavior.   There was some control for this through interviewing librarians in nearby libraries and through previous experience as an interviewer (as a newspaper reporter and
collecting data for a master's thesis).   For instance, there
may be a certain telltale vacuity to interviews in which
everything is described as trouble free.

3.   Social scientists recognize that there is frequently
a discrepancy between expressed attitudes and behavior.
Possible reasons include attitude measures that do not take
into account enough of the variables influencing behavior,
or the fact that people do not live up to their own expectations (see Deutscher, 1970, pp. 38-39).   The researcher
tried to ask questions that would distinguish attitudes from
actions, but some blurring of the two probably was present
in the responses.

4.   It is possible that staff of one or more of the six
libraries not participating would have presented an especially
bleak picture of reference and referral activity.   In two of
the libraries the directors' secretaries described staff shortages, a condition that could adversely affect public service.
Another library did not cooperate because, according to one
librarian on the staff, the librarians were overworked and
angry with the director.   Two libraries were said by their
directors to be little involved in referral activity.   One of
these was in a corporate library, which may not do a lot of

referring, but the other was at a law library in which the director's comments were contradicted to an extent by statements of a librarian on the staff. A staff shortage was mentioned at the law library also. From the sixth library a negative reply was received only via the postcard, with no explanation given as to why it would not participate. This library was criticized, however, by the staff at a nearby library regarding the adequacy of its collection and reference service.

Regarding the theme of staff shortages in four of the six libraries, this could mean that their librarians had less time to make contacts with outside resources, to create card files or other referral aids, or to assist users; and it may have also adversely affected their morale. These types of negative findings are reported in the next chapter, but probably to a lesser degree than if the omitted libraries had been included.

Fortunately at the libraries where interviewing was done it did not seem likely that the researcher was being steered to the "best" reference librarians. In general, reference staffs were not large enough to permit this and still offer three or four interviews in a single day. In the one library with about double the normal number of reference librarians to choose from, the head of reference left the choice up to the researcher. When told in one library that there was not time for an interview with a librarian who was leaving the staff, agreement was reached for a brief interview. In a couple of settings the best performers may have been chosen, however, in that some reference work was performed by nonprofessionals, who were less familiar with some sources, and who were not interviewed.

5. The research primarily sought to identify factors, not to precisely measure them. It was qualitative, not quantitative. Therefore a test for reliabilty (repeatability) was not possible due to insufficient structure for a second researcher to replicate and due to effects of the researcher's personality and relationship to respondents (see Mo, 1978, p. 174). Nor, due to the tentative nature of many of the conclusions, was an attempt made to employ independent measures of the validity of the findings. Readers must judge validity based on their own background and on the cogency of the presentation.

CHAPTER 3

RESULTS

INTRODUCTION

The core of this chapter is a series of brief essays on different factors that the data seemed to indicate influence or at least are related to willingness and ability to refer. The number and variety of factors suggest that the subject of referral is indeed a complex one. At the end of this chapter, however, there is described the central theme of equity, the discussion of which continues in the remaining chapters.

Since one of the purposes of this study was to define referral and good referral, the presentation begins with a definition of referral that has been discerned as a result of this investigation. In Chapter 1 arguments were presented as to why referral could be thought of in quite broad terms. A broad conception was useful during the data gathering phase, but now the need is for precision so that the goal of clarifying this complex issue is reached. There follows a definition of effective referral and, in the succeeding discussion of the quality of efficiency, of efficient referral. Further elaboration of the definition, including discussion of good referral viewed within the context of equity, is saved for the final chapter.

FUNCTIONAL DEFINITIONS OF LIBRARY
REFERRAL AND EFFECTIVE REFERRAL

Defining library referral is difficult. Both dictionary
definitions and that which is defined by actual librarian
practice were found to vary in scope and specific detail.
In light of these complexities, the definition that seems to
capture the essential function of what interviewees described
is as follows:

> Library referral is an act by library employees of
> responding to individuals' needs by directing these
> individuals to another person, or to a place under
> the control of another person, for the fulfillment of
> these needs.

"To refer" in this sense would mean "to respond to individuals' needs by directing these individuals to another person,
or to a place under the control of another person, for the
fulfillment of these needs."

This is a broadening of the meaning of referral found
in an Oxford English Dictionary supplement (Burchfield,
1982): "The referring of an individual to an expert or
specialist for advice; specifically, the directing (usually by
a general practitioner) of a patient to a medical consultant
for specialist treatment." This study's definition is broader
in that it includes the possibility of the user being referred
to a library or other place in which users may find the
needed information on their own, without interacting with a
specialist. One would not expect to go to the office of a
medical specialist, read material there, use diagnostic equip-
ment, and otherwise satisfy one's need on one's own, but
one can visit another library and possibly do all or most of
the information gathering on one's own.

Webster's Third New International Dictionary (1976)
includes the meaning of "the process of directing or redi-
recting (as a medical case, a patient) to an appropriate specialist or agency for definitive treatment," but the unabridged
edition of the Random House Dictionary of the English Language (1966) is much less specific, offering as a definition:
"1. an act of referring, the state of being referred 2.
an instance of referring 3. a person recommended to someone or for something."

If by "referral" is meant simply "an act of referring," referral has not only the meaning of sending a person somewhere, but also sending a thing to a person, or a person to a thing, along with the further meaning of looking at something for information. Thus Webster's Third New International Dictionary states succinctly that "to refer" is "to send or direct for treatment, aid, information, decision (--a student to a dictionary) (--a bill to a committee) (--a patient to a specialist)"; and, for the meaning of looking at something for information, gives the example: "referred to his watch and hurried away."

The last meaning, looking at something, was of course excluded from consideration in this study of library referral. It would be a part of reference, but not referral. Similarly, referring a student to a dictionary in the same department of the library would be part of the reference work process, not referral. To state otherwise is to dilute the meaning of referral to the point at which it is indistinguishable from reference work.

In Chapter 1 the question of whether interlibrary loan or telephoning to obtain an answer to a user's question is referral was left open. If "referring a bill to a committee" is referral, might sending a loan request to a library be also? The Oxford English Dictionary (Murray, 1910) includes as a definition of refer: "to commit, submit, hand over (a question, cause or matter) to some special or ultimate authority for consideration, decision, execution, etc.," with the example, "Socrates proposes at last to refer the question to some older person." If referral is an act of referring, could telephoning an expert for an answer to a reference question also be considered a referral?

While forwarding a request to fill a need is similar to directing people to have their needs filled, there is a basic difference, which in the end makes it clearer to reserve the word "referral" for instances of directing the person. The difference is one of responsibility. In referring people, the librarian is responsible for making an accurate referral, but the people are then responsible for obtaining the information on their own, or a person to whom a user is referred is responsible once he or she agrees to help the user. In sending or telephoning an interlibrary loan or reference request, librarians or their institution remain partially responsible for seeing that the transaction is completed. Interlibrary loan must be considered just that, similar in some ways to referral, but not referral. Likewise telephoning another library for an answer cannot be excluded from this study because of its close relationship to referral, but for purposes of conceptual clarity it cannot be called referral. It is also not quite the same as "consulting," unless the calling librarian just wants to be told how to approach looking for an answer so that the request is only for advice and not for the complete answer.

Those interviewed were asked for their definition of referral, and several stated that both directing a user to another location and calling for an answer to a reference question are types of referral. These responses may have been caused in part by familiarity with the expression, "reference referral," which has been used to mean calling a higher level library in a network for reference assistance (the less ambiguous term, "cooperative reference," has also been employed). A few librarian respondents felt that interlibrary loan was a type of referral, and several more were undecided on this point. One academic librarian made the distinction made here, stating that interlibrary loan is not referral because her library was "still handling" the request, while referral is "making the requester go out and do more work."

Librarians generally agreed that referrals could be made in the sense of sending someone elsewhere within the same library, as well as out of the library. This distinction can be termed "intra-library" referral versus "extra-library" referral. If the user is referred to a coworker or to another department where a coworker would be expected to answer a question if asked, it would be an intra-library referral.

Two interviewees in the same academic library thought of referral only in the most narrow sense. One stated that he "never used the word," which to him has an "almost medical" meaning. The other commented: "I think when you say 'referral' you're really referring to something in a more professional service, at least that's what springs to mind: a doctor's referring a patient, a practitioner referring his patient to a specialist."

It may be this medical model which influenced Childers. As mentioned in Chapter 1, in a 1980 article Childers made a distinction between "steering"--simply providing directions to another resource, and "referring"--actually trying to make contact for the client (p. 928). While the data for this dissertation were being analyzed, Childers' book, Information & Referral: Public Libraries, (1983) was published. "Referral" for the data gathering stage of the study reported in the book was defined by asking, "Does the staff actively help the public make contact with an outside resource, by making an appointment, calling an agency, etc?" (p. 16). Only 17 percent of libraries identified as information and referral providers offered referral in this sense as a standard service (p. 26).

In distinction from Childers' usage, under the definition of referral arrived at here the librarian does not have to make contact for the user in order for a referral to have occurred. Indeed, the person referred may obtain the needed information or material in the place referred to without direct contact being made with any individual. Also, as explained, if the librarian makes contact for the purpose of obtaining the desired information or material for the user, it is an instance of cooperative reference or interlibrary loan, not referral.

Since so far the definition proposed in this study says nothing about the accuracy of referral, a definition of potentially effective library referral will now be offered. The word "potentially" is included because determining that the referral was in fact effective would require feedback from the place referred to or from the individual referred. With "effective" defined in Webster's Third New International Dictionary as "able to accomplish a purpose," and with library referral discerned to have the definition indicated, the notion of effective library referral may be defined as follows:

> Potentially effective library referral is an act by library employees of responding to individuals' needs by directing these individuals to another person, or to a place under the control of another person, thought to be able to fulfill these needs.

This is a definition in terms of advancing the welfare of the user. As will be brought out later, other people

involved in the referral process may have additional objec-
tives that may conflict with the goal of satisfying the needs
of the user, so that determining what is an effective referral process depends to some extent on one's point of view.
The ability and the desire to be effective in the referral
situation are influenced by factors to be delineated in this
chapter.

MAJOR FACTORS RELATED TO LIBRARY REFERRAL

The primary purpose of this study was to suggest the
factors that influence library referral. Described first are
six personal qualities, followed by factors relating to the
potential referrer's library, outside resources, and the user.
While the considerable detail provided in the discussion of
the last three areas demonstrates how varied referral related
settings and interactions can be, the final paragraph or
paragraphs of the description of factors in these areas provide brief summaries.

Personal Qualities as Factors

Six personality traits affecting referral behavior were
distinguished in examining the interview transcripts. The
names of these traits are effficiency, equity, achievement
motivation, empathy, tact, and independence. They appeared to varying degrees to affect the behavior of the librarians and those with whom they interacted, and their
influence will be noted in the succeeding discussions of
factors relating to the librarian's own library, outside resources, and clientele. While each of the six is defined and
discussed separately below, two or more are commonly observed acting in various combinations of concert or contra-
diction.

Efficiency

As expressed by Webster's Third New International
Dictionary, efficiency is the "capacity to produce desired
results with a minimum of expenditure of energy, time,
money or materials." In terms of referral, this means action
that is effective, but also efficient in that waste is avoided.
A further definition of referral, that of potentially efficient
referral, is possible:

> Potentially efficient library referral is an act by li-
> brary employees of responding to individuals' needs
> by directing these individuals to another person,
> or to a place under the control of another person,
> thought to be able to fulfill these needs and ap-
> proachable without unnecessary loss of these indi-
> viduals' energy, time, money, or materials.

Again, the user's point of view is assumed in this definition,
but in a particular interaction with a user librarians may
think in terms of what conserves their own or their library's
resources in addition to what is efficient for the user.
Thus librarians deciding whether a student should be referred may decide on the basis not only of how much effort
would be required of the user but also how much effort
would be required of them in making the referral.

In general, librarians interviewed were concerned that
their own time and the time of other librarians and users
not be wasted. They did not want to be required to do
work that they considered to be unnecessary, and they appreciated training, helpful coworkers, and other elements
that expedited their reference and referral work. At times
there was disagreement regarding what would be efficient,
as seen for example, in the differing views regarding whether one's own collection should be nearly self-sufficient or
merely a starting place for referral elsewhere. At other
times lapses in efficiency were discerned, as in the frequent
inability to provide travel directions to the resources of
nearby institutions.

Equity

The meaning of equity intended in this chapter is as
expressed by McClintock and Keil (1982):

> Equity, in its most generic sense, refers to those
> decision rules that humans employ to define how and
> when a just and fair distribution of valued resources
> obtains between actors. The rules themselves may
> be more or less codified, and may be quite general
> or specific to a particular relationship. The value
> of the resources distributed may be positive or nega-
> tive, that is, they may be rewarding or punishing

to the participants. The resources themselves may
represent activities, physical commodities, affective
states, or any other valued condition. Thus, for
example, one may afford another a positive resource
by verbally expressing love, presenting a gift, or
changing a tire. [p. 338]

The authors continue: "Defining what is fair or equitable
has been and continues to be a principal activity of human
actors who are dependent upon one another, that is, inter-
dependent, in terms of valued outcomes" (p. 338).

However, in one field "equity" has a more narrow
meaning, McClintock and Keil explain:

In social psychology a somewhat different and
more specific definition of equity dominates most
contemporary research and theory. Beginning with
Homans' notion of distributive justice (1961), and
including its formalization by Adams (1965), equity
has been defined as one of several specific rules
that may be employed to determine what is a fair
distribution of outcomes. Namely, the rule of equity
asserts that one's outcome should be proportional
to one's input or contribution. [p. 338]

Leventhal (1980) also reports that "most equity researchers
have equated the term with a type of justice based on merit
or contributions" (p. 29). He suggests that the words
"contributions rule" be applied to equity in the "more narrow sense of justice that is based on matching of rewards
to contributions" (p. 29). Leventhal introduces his terminol-
ogy because

close inspection of the writings of equity theorists
suggests they do sometimes use the term in a broad
sense, as well as the narrow. However, they do
not differentiate between the two usages, and may
slide casually from one to the other. [p. 29]

Findings and theories of social psychologists regarding equity
will be presented in the next chapter.

Both efficiency and equity pervade the referral process.
The librarian weighs both the effort required and the effort

owed with respect to dealings with users, outsiders (those
whom the library does not have a specific responsibility to
serve), outside contacts (people outside the library who
are able to assist in providing needed information or materials and with whom the librarian is on friendly terms), coworkers (fellow workers in the same library), and the library director. At times a lapse in efficiency can be explained as an expression of the equity principle. Thus,
that librarians were found to be poorly prepared to give
specific travel directions to other libraries is more under-
standable if one considers that handouts showing routes to
other libraries might raise fears of inequitable overuse of
these libraries.

Achievement Motivation

This term was chosen through a literature search after the data was gathered to describe one aspect of what
was observed. Expressions that came naturally to mind,
such as "pride in work," did not seem as exact or are not
as widespread in the psychological literature. Spence and
Helmreich (1983) note that achievement motivation posits "a
stable dispositional tendency to strive towards performance
excellence--a tendency whose strength varies from one individual to another" (p. 65). These authors state that the
motive to achieve has traditionally been conceptualized as a
unitary dimension, but claim to have identified three relatively independent factors: "mastery (the preference for challenging tasks and for meeting internal standards of performance), work (the desire to work hard and to do a good
job), and competitiveness (the enjoyment of interpersonal
competition and the desire to do better than others)" (p.
65). The mastery and work factors were apparent in the
statements of some of the librarians interviewed. The third
factor, competitiveness, no doubt is a motivator for some
librarians, but it was not expressed in the interviews.

The desire to work hard and to do a good job is seen
in a public library reference head's opinion of what motivates
referral:

> I think a personal feeling that you have about your
> job. Do you want to get people out of the library
> with some kind of answer, or do you want to give
> them the answer to whatever the question is and

make sure it's the answer? If you feel unsatisfied
you haven't given the answer, haven't referred the
question on, then you will refer.

This desire is seen in the length some librarians go to find
answers. An academic librarian mentioned making an after
work visit to a police department to obtain needed data. A
public librarian related a series of calls in an attempt to find
out "why is there a green light over the police station?"
She noted: "We were calling around, but finally had to
give up. They did give up on that one." The failure
"still bothers me to this day," she stated.

Achievement motivation may lead to an inefficient use
of time if librarians insist on finding answers without help
from others. Complained one reference head:

> [Coworker] is one of those people who will turn a
> question that can be easily answered into an exer-
> cise. People don't want that. Information USA
> gives you a name you can call of a subject special-
> ist, and just using that will get you an answer in
> half an hour that she'll spend half a day with. It's
> good for her, bad for us. Very satisfying for [co-
> worker] to find an answer.

Less challenging questions can be less satisfying. Said an
academic librarian who enjoyed online computer bibliographic
searching:

> I get only moderate satisfaction from teaching a stu-
> dent how to use Engineering Index. I really like
> for someone ... to call and say I've got a hundred
> dollars to spend [for computer time] on all aspects
> of liquified natural gas. I don't like to stop when
> hot on the trail because the money's run out. I like
> the detective work.

One further class of comments can be related to
achievement motivation: those pertaining to limits on or a
lack of such motivation. Several librarians spoke quite
frankly of personal limitations. An academic librarian said:

> Sometimes you just get fed up and just say: "I know
> where the answer is. I can really put out for this

kid, but I'm just pooped, and I'm not going to go
beyond the cursory, you know, where to look for
the information."

Another librarian said of McClure and Hernon's (1983) finding of a lack of referral (see p. 2 above): "That's probably an attitude problem. They don't want to be bothered.... Government documents is awfully mind boggling
for a lot of people to deal with." Achievement motivation,
then, impels the librarian to perform well, and its absence
can cause inadequacy in reference and referral service.

Empathy

According to Batson and Coke (1981), empathy is "an
emotional response elicited by and congruent with the perceived welfare of someone else" (p. 169). This definition
will be accepted here. These authors state that their reason for prefering the term empathy to that of sympathy to
describe "congruent emotion elicited by witnessing another
in distress in a helping situation" is that "it has typically
been the term used by social psychologists during the past
decade" (p. 170).

The finding of this study is that referral practice of
librarians seemed to be less affected by their feelings of
empathy than by their sense of equity. Still, empathy was
expressed by some interviewees. One librarian will be referred to as the "Exemplary Referrer" because of an especially high degree of apparent knowledge and ability pertaining to referral. This librarian described reference as "de-
tective" work, as did the online searcher quoted in regard
to achievement motivation, but added an expression of empathy for the user:

> I like the detective quality of reference, and I enjoy
> learning new things, so to me it's a challenge. I
> get bored at the end of the day because I think if
> I have to use "Psych" Abstracts one more time I'll
> scream. I mean that's part of the job because
> there's a certain repetition.
> I like the interaction with the students. I enjoy
> the bright ones. I enjoy the ones that are slow that
> you can bring up to a good level and you see them
> grasping.

Other expressions of empathy for users included that of a law librarian who often felt "badly" having to refer students because she could "see by the look on their faces that they are on the verge of having a breakdown" since they "don't have the time." While there were only a few expressions of such feelings, they may be a common contributor to service.

Tact

Tact, according to <u>Webster's Third New International Dictionary</u>, is "a keen sense of what to do or say in a difficult or delicate situation in order to maintain good relations with others to avoid offense." It seemed to be especially important in dealings with coworkers, with whom interaction was necessary on a continuing basis. The absence of tact might have caused resentment, which in turn could limit friendly interaction and the sharing of knowledge.

Tact was also important in dealings with other libraries. Without the use of tact in asking for assistance others may be less likely to provide aid, and if a person does not display tact in providing help, the individual receiving it may be less likely to seek it in the future. For example, a librarian described how those telephoning a backup library (a library responsible for helping other libraries in a formal network) were curtly asked why some common reference work had not been checked first. Such treatment can cause hesitancy to telephone the backup library thereafter. Similarly librarians were likely to maintain some level of tact while assisting users and frequently expected like consideration in return.

Independence

As defined in <u>Webster's New International Dictionary</u> independence is the state of "not looking to others for one's opinions or for the guidance of one's conduct," with the further meaning possible of "marked by impatience with or annoyance at restriction." The independence cited by participants in the study centered on their willingness to break regulations in order to assist users.

A head of reference told of conflict with the library director, who was asking for a reduction in long distance

telephoning to obtain answers to reference questions. In
another case a public librarian had been told at various
times to spend no more than fifteen minutes or half an hour
on questions, but he "frequently" spent much more because
reference work

> is the main thing that gives a tremendous amount of
> pleasure. If I had to deal with each question in a
> perfunctory manner or desultory manner, I would be
> extremely unhappy on the job. I've spent over a
> day on a question.

A reference head at a small public library, constrained by
network rules to make most referrals to a first-level backup
library, would try to bypass the backup library if it seemed
unlikely that it could answer a question using its own resources. This person stated:

> I'm not afraid to ask. I'm an outgoing person. If
> I'm told I can't do it, I will backtrack and go thru
> [designated backup library]. I'm not afraid to make
> an attempt.

Independence in this sense of disregarding policy was not
as likely to be part of reference and referral as are equity,
efficiency, achievement motivation, and tact because in most
instances policies were not objected to.

   Independence in the sense of having considerable freedom in the handling of tasks was more common, however.
In general, librarians interviewed seemed to be in the situation described by the public librarian who, while conceding
that referral depends in part on whether it is "highly
stressed in departmental policy," nonetheless concluded,
"Because of what I see as the nature of reference work, the
librarian handling the question, I think, is the key factor."
That is to say, reference and referral in most libraries offers the librarian considerable independence in deciding how
to handle a particular query.

Summary of Personal Qualities

   The six personal qualities identified--achievement
motivation, efficiency, empathy, equity, independence, and
tact--are likely to be found to at least some extent in most

people. Since this was a study based on interviews with reference librarians, examples of the six qualities are composed primarily of their reports of their own behavior. However, there were suggestions that others involved in the referral act, including the director, the user, coworkers, and outsiders also possessed these qualities. Most are likely to exhibit some signs of eagerness to achieve, tact in interpersonal relations, empathy, striving towards efficiency, concern for equity, and preference for acting independently at one time or another.

The six qualities, while they may sound like positive attributes, are not a simple list of virtues to be cultivated by the librarian who wishes to increase or improve referral. They may encourage or discourage referral, depending on how they are applied. For example, efficiency may dictate that a particular referral may be too time consuming, independence may lead to the ignoring of a library policy to refer, and tact may keep a librarian from suggesting a referral when a coworker fails to suggest it. Still, all six qualities are capable of facilitating referral.

These qualities were not of equal importance in the findings. Equity is the primary theme. Empathy was not frequently described by librarians, but references to it have added importance because they help to counterbalance the prevailing equity perspective, especially in regard to service to users. Tact also was not described much by interviewees. The assumption of its importance is based partly on comments and partly on the belief that the level of mutual assistance described would be impossible in its absence.

While equity, empathy, and tact are mainly concerned with dealings with others, efficiency, achievement motivation, and independence are more centered on the self. Like equity, efficiency is a major theme. It does not have the complexity or the impact of equity because the conclusion that efficiency would be a consideration at work is hardly new information. The way the question, "Efficient for whom?," is answered by different conceptions of equity does require deeper analysis, however. Achievement motivation as a concept is closely related to efficiency. Its inclusion is based on several participants' comments, plus the assumption that people who strive to do a good job are motivated in part by something like achievement motivation. Independence in the

sense of willingness to disobey authority appeared to be an
important factor for a few librarians.

Obviously the six personal qualities are interrelated.
For example, in terms of the central theme of equity, being
tactful and receiving tactful treatment in return is equitable.
The more emotional quality of empathy complements the more
cognitive equity. Being efficient is equitable in that someone's resources are not wasted, but it may also be inequitable in that someone else's resources are utilized instead.
Lack of achievement motivation in a librarian is inequitable
to the library and its users. Allowing people the independence that is their due is equitable. Many other connections
could be drawn. Achievement motivation or empathy for the
user could lead to a display of independence in circumvent-
ing rules in order to aid the user. Tact may be viewed as
a means to achievement. Proceeding according to empathy
rather than to equity could be considered to be inefficient.

In summary, the description and analysis to follow can
be read mainly in terms of equity. Efficiency as a secondary
focus helps to make many connections also. Other personal
qualities add detail but are a lesser part of the picture.

Factors Concerning the Potential
Referrer's Library

Characteristics of the interviewees' own libraries were
significant in providing incentives and support for referral.
Included in this section are the influences of the director,
coworkers, training and experience, work load at the reference desk, collection strength, and printed referral aids.
As in other sections, it is difficult to separate referral from
reference work in general so there is some overlap with the
latter.

Interaction with the Director

At the top of a library's administrative hierarchy is
the director. Despite the importance of this position, many
interviewees did not mention their director as a source of
influence on their referral practices. Moreover, some of the
comments that were made were strongly negative. Only negative comments about the influence of the director on the

referral process were heard at three of the ten formally
chosen library sites where interviewing was conducted.
Only positive comments were heard at two of these libraries,
and both positive and negative from another. The remaining four libraries produced no comments. Comments from
librarians at three libraries approached informally were all
negative.

Points raised by librarians on this issue fit well with
the qualities of equity and efficiency. Thus a librarian
who had quit her job at one library said a cause of bad
referral would be poor morale, and poor morale

> has a lot to do with how much your work is appre-
> ciated by your supervisor or director. It has a lot
> to do with, personally, how important they view
> you, not just as a reference librarian, but as a
> person.

This librarian felt a lack of equity in terms of not receiving
the recognition she felt was her due. She also felt the director created inefficiency by being too involved in routine
operations:

> [The director] is personally involved in every as-
> pect and function of the library. He looks at and
> examines everything, and if he decides that [another
> library] might have it ... we have to make a direct
> phone call. [Question: Is he often right?] No,
> usually this ends up being busy work.

In a second library a librarian who had been having
"running battles" with her director described how she had
been formally reprimanded for not, in the director's opinion,
following his instructions regarding a telephone request to
a backup library. In the same library another librarian
told how, due to the director's strict insistence on using a
backup library, he felt obliged to forward requests for the
source of even trite quotations:

> When I do call in to [backup library] I will say,
> "You probably won't find this but--," and then I
> tell them I have to call anyway. [Question: You
> say this apologetically?] Yeah, because if I don't
> and the person complains, then my head rolls.

These librarians saw their director as creating inefficiencies
by being too concerned with service owed the user. Again,
in a library in which the staff refused the director's suggestion that they participate in the interviewing for this
study, an informant said that the reason was that they felt
overworked by the director.

In a fourth library the director received both positive
and negative comments. One librarian made the general
statement: "Our director is very much with us. We do our
work, and he respects us as professionals, and we don't
have anyone breathing down our necks." Relating more directly to referral, another librarian complained about the
procedure for obtaining a pass granting access to another
library from the director: "You're supposed to chase him,
and if he's in a good mood he gives you the card, and that
kind of thing, which I think is a very inconvenient system."

At a fifth library, the senior reference librarian complained that the director showed too little interest:

> Almost a laissez-faire attitude that can contribute to
> dissatisfaction because we rarely, rarely get any
> feedback on our performance, whether it's good or
> bad. We rarely see him, period.

She added: "I find it difficult to ask my boss for help.
He's not really very approachable.... He's very busy."

In a sixth library the head of reference stated that
referral is "one aspect of the library that the administration
in general is not aware of, or just vaguely aware of the
significance of it and the importance of it." This she indicated could be due to a lack of pressure on the director
from users, who might be concerned about referral but "not
vociferous in it." In the same library another librarian refused to be interviewed, questioning the need for the research and suggesting that someone "should do a study of
library administrators making arbitrary decisions."

A seventh library's director, declining to participate
in the study, gave as a reason a lack of referral made by
his library. he also said he was not familiar with the access
policies of nearby university libraries and considered reaching them by public transportation to be complicated. Later,

a source in the library said that referrals were made frequently and that using public transportation to reach the
university libraries was easy. One possible explanation for
this conflict in opinions is that the director had little interest in referral.

An eighth library's director, by contrast, was said
by one of his librarians to give referral a higher priority
because he "comes from a reference background, and has a
strong bent to reference services." Only in the ninth library were a few specific examples cited regarding the way
the director had promoted referral.

In summary, several respondent librarians complained
of not being appreciated, of being forced to follow inefficient referral practices, and of being overworked by over-
zealous directors. Some librarians, in short, felt they were
being treated inequitably, although the directors probably
felt they were only doing what was equitable for the users.
A couple of library directors were accused of having too
little interest in reference and referral, which the librarians
probably saw as shortchanging the users, although some
realization was expressed that the director had many other
duties, and that referral was not an issue regarding which
the public applied much pressure. The main positive comments concerned a director who was not "breathing down
our necks," and one who had taken several steps to facilitate or to publicize reference and referral.

Interaction with Coworkers

Librarians for the most part described coworkers as
helpful, whether when referred to, or when asked for advice
regarding reference or referral. Positive relationships with
coworkers that seemed to affect referral will be described
first, followed by negative ones.

Academic librarians were about three times more likely
than public librarians to include referral to coworkers in
their definition of referral. This is in part due to the
academic libraries being more likely to have an advanced
degree in a subject speciality, and also to the academic libraries studied being a bit more likely to have separate subject specialities in different parts of the building. Public
librarians were more likely to say that they consulted a
more experienced coworker.

The coworker asked for help is not always a reference
librarian. It may be a cataloger who, as in one case, was
a "baseball fanatic." It might not even be a librarian. A
librarian formerly employed at a publishing house had called
technical editors for help. In one public library, nonprofessionals were scheduled at the reference desk during less
busy periods, and the comment was made that "there are
library assistants who've been on the staff longer than some
of the professionals in the department, and it's not at all
unusual for that professional to ask that person, 'Gee, do
you know anything that's going to help with this?'" In
another public library a nonprofessional provided driving
directions when people were referred to various locations.

Some librarians told of a very open atmosphere, with
no hesitation in asking a coworker for advice. A librarian
with comparatively little experience, working at a large library, said he had only a "vague notion" of several specialized libraries in the area, including a law library:

> I don't know where it is and I've never referred
> anybody there because when we get a legal question
> we usually powwow in the back, and then somebody
> says, "Oh, I'll give them the phone number." It
> just hasn't been me. I haven't looked it up. I
> should.

In another library, checking with another librarian was portrayed as a learning experience:

> Sometimes I know the answer. I think that's the
> correct answer, but I still ask [business librarian],
> and many times I might learn something--"Oh, in
> addition to this, [business librarian] knows this
> source," so it's a learning experience, so in that
> sense I'm referring. I'm improving my own refer-
> ence techniques, right?

An additional way in which questions get turned over to
fellow reference librarians is through the practice of passing
unfinished questions to the next person on duty at the reference desk, so in a sense one receives help in finishing a
question without having to ask.

Tact and equity considerations are evident in intralibrary

referrals. Two librarians mentioned telephoning a colleague in another part of the building to ask something like, "Is this a good time for you?," before sending the user. This demonstrates consideration for both the colleague and the user. On rare occasions librarians may even be called at home. While this indicates respect for the librarian's expertise, and the head of one small public library's reference department stressed that she had told her coworkers that she could be called at home, it can also be perceived to be an imposition. Said one academic librarian:

> You try not to do it because you don't want to bother the people, but I've done it, and people have called me, and sometimes it's no more than, "Will you be in tomorrow because the student would like to set up an appointment." I do that when I know the answer is here, and the student is there and can only be there at that moment, say an evening student.

There is a danger that tact may become timidity. One librarian suggested that if a coworker were checking a union list for a periodical and

> they couldn't find it because the spelling was wrong, you know, with the patron looking and two or three people, and you're there next to it--you know the answer--there is a tendency that you wouldn't correct it. Sometimes the librarian would say: "Hmm, I couldn't find it. [Coworker] would you try"-- which has been our attitude sometimes. Then I would be more willing to--"Hey, it's 'ie' instead of 'ei'," and they would appreciate this kind of interaction to provide the correct answer.

This particular librarian felt that the utmost tact was owed a coworker, even at the expense of the user.

While not directly related to reference or referral, the following comments by one librarian about conversations with coworkers reflect the strength of the friendships and caring that may develop:

> We do a lot of that here, among the staff, and [coworker] can be less formal, more open, too, but

> especially with some of the other women. We do
> constant analyzing of ourselves and how we feel
> about patrons and our work.... The morale in the
> library is good. The people are all interested in
> their jobs.

And further:

> I like being in a nonacademic library. I like the
> pop psychology stuff and all that. This is a won-
> derful job for me, and I'm very happy with the good
> library. I care a great deal about many members of
> the staff, and I sit right here in the middle of the
> community, which is my community--see my friends
> all day, meet new people. It's wonderful.

Interviewing did not produce the opposite of the above passage. Other librarians expressed some dissatisfaction, but
no one made a negative generalization about both job duties
and coworkers.

    Between the attitudes of interdependence and distrust
is the situation of the librarian who did not admit to much
dependence on her more experienced supervisor: "I do a
lot of thinking out loud. I tell [supervisor] what I'm looking for. I work very independently, but talk out loud."
The same librarian described how at a library she had
worked at previously she gave advice without being asked:
"We sat at desks and the phones kept ringing, so I sort of
overheard. If I had a suggestion, I made it."

    Another aspect of asking for help is the influence of
status. One supervisor stated of two coworkers:

> They're somewhat lower in status, so they're sup-
> posed to be a help to me. I don't take advantage
> of that. It makes it easier for me to ask people for
> help. They don't have the right to say no.

    This discussion now turns from its basically positive
orientation to the negative findings of not trusting coworkers, or not being trusted. Most often this distrust was directed against nonprofessionals, who were specifically assigned to reference work, or who were the only people available to answer questions when the reference desk is closed,

or who simply are approached by the public and give answers despite the availability of reference librarians.

In one academic library, reference coverage

> depends on who is available, which can range from
> zero to quite good. A lot of hours are covered only
> by students, but we have some very good graduate
> students. Some of them can find government docu-
> ments.

In another academic library it was said of nighttime assistants at the reference desk that "sometimes they haven't
understood the question, much less provided proper answers." In an academic library in which nonprofessionals
were not assigned to the reference desk, one librarian said
he had "objected bitterly" when he found a student assistant
attempting to give reference help but giving incorrect information.

In public libraries, mention was made of nonprofessional librarian assistants making incorrect referrals to the
library's documents department, and of nonprofessionals in
branches calling in questions "that they could find it an
almanac." A supervisor in a public library stressed that
there was a wide range in the performance of nonprofessionals in branches:

> Some of them will just be very unwilling to let any-
> one go out the door without the question answered,
> or without getting the information.... Someone else
> will--"No, we don't have it," and be sort of reluc-
> tant to take it any further.

At times feelings against nonprofessionals seem inequitable. A public librarian described an earlier time in
her library when

> there were librarians who were very conscious of
> their status as librarians.... They didn't want any
> clerical person to answer a question of any--of
> course there are questions they can't answer and
> shouldn't try, but I mean little things like, "The
> newspaper is over there." Something like that.

Another public librarian gave a bitter portrayal of her own earlier experience as a nonprofessional in a small branch academic library:

> The librarian was a bit like many male librarians, and prided himself on his position. He was a doctor, and would tell me not to play librarian, because of course I didn't even have a master's then....
> The fact that I was there when he wasn't, and I was running the place when he wasn't, didn't matter.

Occasionally interviewees were critical of fellow professionals, with several librarians expressing the opinion that subject specialists were sometimes reluctant or inept when staffing the general reference desk. As one academic librarian said, they

> aren't as aware as the rest of us are who normally are in the reference room as to where to look for the material, so some of them wing it or fake it. Others just say, "Come back when the other people are here."

The indifferent attitude of a coworker at one time made a public librarian very upset, so that he told him

> that he'd been on the job so long and didn't help people any more. I learned from [coworker] to do more for the person. He would just sit there and point. Used to irritate the hell out of me.

Another librarian gave the following succinct reply to the question of why he might not refer to a coworker:

> I could be really vague here. Relationships between individual departments, or hierarchical relationships, or just not thinking a possible referral will be handled adequately.

There was only one instance of a librarian telling how she had been the object of distrust. In an earlier position in a library in which contacting other libraries was not encouraged, she had been accused of taking personal telephone calls one time when she was called back by an outside librarian she had telephoned a request to.

More often librarians admitted to hesitating to ask a
coworker a question for fear they would appear foolish.
Said one:

> Sure I feel a little uncomfortable. I think first:
> "Is this a silly question? Can I answer it myself?"
> My first month here maybe I did spend too much
> time on a question. I think most people do that,
> until they realize that you can ask silly questions
> and everybody does it.

Similarly a public librarian felt that referrals were not as
frequent as they might be because "older librarians at
branches didn't admit failing." In another public library a
reference head remembered a "a very proud black man" as
one who: "wanted to do it all himself. [I] had to beg,
plead: 'It's not a private office downstairs. Just walk in
and ask.'"

In summary, librarians commonly ask coworkers for
necessary help. When such requests occur and are well received and responded to, it is equitable for all concerned:
the user's need is met, the asking librarian receives considerate assistance, the librarians asked receive the respect
due their expertise, and outside librarians are not bothered
with requests that should have been answered in-house.
That the very tact or friendliness that makes it easy to
make demands of a coworker can be extended too far, however, is seen in the librarian who was afraid to correct a
coworker's error.

Nonprofessionals may be inadequately trained for reference work, or may try to assist users even when expected
not to. Some do quite well with training and experience,
and some professionals' disdain towards them seems unjusti-
fied. Perhaps librarians feel their status and the value of
their training is lessened when nonprofessionals do work
similar to their own. The most common complaint about professionals, on the other hand, was that in academic libraries
some subject specialists would prefer to be consulted only
or to receive referrals, rather than having to help at times
at the general reference desk.

Finally, the service due the user and the efficiency
owed the library can be hampered by a hesitancy to admit

ignorance. The best safeguard against this seems to be to
promote a friendly atmosphere in which librarians commonly
consult with one another.

Extent of Training and Experience

In-service training in reference and referral was
found in this study to be informal and low-keyed, and librarians reported no cause to complain of being too closely
supervised in this respect. In fact, a few complained of
too little guidance.

One academic librarian said she had never been told
how much to do for users and felt frustrated until she had
assimilated this knowledge through observation. In the
same library, a supervisor stated that an attempt to formu-
late a written reader services policy had been abandoned
because there were too many variables.

In another academic library, a supervisor described a
typical situation when asked if referral were a matter of
policy. She said that there was no written policy, and that
she had never discussed the matter with the director, but
that she knew he wanted a satisfied clientele. When a new
librarian joined the staff, she gave "more orientation than
training," mentioning to them that her "philosophy of librarianship" was "to never send somebody away completely
empty handed."

Nor were training and policy guidance regarding referral much emphasized in public libraries. The reference
head at a backup library said the approach there was to
"feel your way, and try to do what you feel is the sensible,
intelligent thing." He confessed that a "less casual" approach might be preferable, yet he himself disagreed with
another supervisor regarding the extent to which requests
should be made to a higher-level backup library. At another
public library, a librarian said as to whether there was a
referral policy in writing that "probably something possibly
is because the library does tend to try to cover everything
with policies." As to whether she had been given instruction, she commented:

> I really can't remember. I think I just sort of know
> what's acceptable here, and what isn't and what is

appropriate referral, and it's something I really haven't thought of.

At the same public library, the head of reference confessed that training was "less formal" than he would like; and noted that, with a small staff, training that is too formal does not seem justified, but "if a training program is too informal, it may be given a very low priority." Still, he seemed relatively well organized:

I work with new staff for a number of months after they join the library. We talk about individuals that I know in various institutions. Whenever possible we try to get them out to meet those individuals.... For some staff members we've actually sent them to the area library or various institutions to go see what facilities are available.

While it seems likely that the dissemination of written policies is an aid to referral training, at several sites it was said explicitly that referral is a subject not requiring a written policy. In a small academic library an interviewee who was not sure if there was a written referral policy felt that "it isn't a big problem here because it's primarily sending people to the local public library for something like Sports Illustrated or Vogue." As the interview progressed, however, he thought of a number of other types of referral that he engaged in. In another academic library the absence of a formal policy was explained by the fact that "a policy is written around here in a negative context: a problem has arisen, a misunderstanding." Likewise, in a public library, a written policy was not considered necessary for a candid reason:

I think you mostly think of policies in terms of areas where you're going to have conflict, perhaps with the patron.... It doesn't seem unreasonable to them that we're not serving them.

In general, librarians did not remember referral being emphasized in their library school training either. Said one:

I don't recall it being a major topic of discussion, and when it did come up it was generally in the context of utilizing other library resources in some

sort of network, for example, not necessarily in
terms of using non-library institutions, or private
individuals, or businesses.

A public librarian did say that in library school she had in
effect "majored" in referral by taking two courses and some
independent studies relating to it, but it was mainly in
terms of referral to agencies, in the traditional sense of
"information and referral."

If professional librarians must largely train themselves
with regard to referral, what of nonprofessionals who must
handle reference and referral? In the section on attitudes
about coworkers, impatience with nonprofessionals' lack of
expertise was cited, although it was also noted that with
sufficient experience some nonprofessionals can rival professionals in ability.

In one particular public library, a supervisor said
that reference workshops were held for all the nonprofessionals who handled reference in the branch libraries. She
observed that "quite often they do something that's not
procedure, and we'll just call them up and tell them, 'Please
do it this way the next time,' but you don't want to establish a bad relationship." Further emphasizing the importance
of being tactful, she stated:

> You can really intimidate someone ... if you start
> saying, "Well, did you ask the person this, and did
> you--," and make them feel that they should have
> done a better interview; and, "Did you check this
> source, and did you check that source?"

In other instances the training of nonprofessionals did
not seem to be as well attended to. Asked whether his staff
knew how to make referrals to lawyers, a law library supervisor said that his reference librarians knew, but he would
have to look into whether nonprofessionals who dealt with
the public did also. An academic library reference head
said she had given a briefing on reference sources several
years ago to the clerks at the reference desk who handled
reference at night, and "perhaps" she should do it again.

The most awareness of training for and policies regarding referral was evidenced by a librarian having knowledge

of a library network committee that was studying the issue.
The committee was writing procedures, this person said,
whereby a new librarian could "see what the referral process is, what you should do in referring your question, and
what kind of information you should have available to give
to the next librarian." The fact that such procedures have
not been written in individual libraries is likely due in part
to referral not being as central a concern in these settings
as it is for a network.

Contrary to the general trend of limited on-the-job
training, one interviewee had received thorough training in
a previous position in a specialized library known for its
collection and telephone service. He recalled:

> The head librarian is really crackerjack in terms of
> training you, and when you share the desk with her
> she watches you like a hawk when you're new, but
> when I goofed up she didn't really lambast me. She
> would actually encourage me to ask questions. Here
> you don't get that, see. Pretty much you're left to
> your own devices, which is kind of bad.

While such careful training was not a common experience,
several librarians did mention being influenced by supervisors or coworkers. Most noteworthy of these comments
was that of a librarian already identified in this dissertation
as the "Exemplary Referrer" due to knowledge and opinions
she expressed. Of her former reference supervisor she
stated:

> She's an excellent reference librarian.... I don't
> think I would have been as good or felt as comfort-
> able in what I was doing if I hadn't had a role
> model, if she hadn't been so helpful those first
> couple of years.

Besides training received, a librarian's reference and
referral behavior is likely to be influenced by the specific
job assignment. One interviewee noted that a previous
position as an interlibrary loan librarian had made it necessary
for her to attend meetings and become knowledgeable about
other libraries. Another former interlibrary loan librarian
said that he was more likely to call a research library for
reference assistance because he had become used to calling

when handling interlibrary loans. Of course, the present
job category was seen as being even more influential. A
current interlibrary loan librarian said that she finds it
"difficult to remember that her library has an extensive
documents collection, and that they are so extensive in what
they cover." On the other hand, she stated, "I will suggest to students the possibility of ILL, whereas another librarian might not do it as quickly as I would." One academic librarian said that he had worked previously in a
large public library that gave substantial reference help by
telephone, and as a result devoted "a little more time to
outside users' requests than some of the other librarians
will."

A further way seen as becoming familiar with other
libraries was to have been employed at them. A librarian
made referrals "a lot" to a university because she had
worked in two of its libraries and "knows what's there."
Knowing people was seen as being at least as important as
knowing collections. A librarian who went from a job at
one library to a job at another said that despite disharmony
that had previously existed between the two libraries,
"there was never any problem because I was familiar with
them."

Formal course work was seen to be a factor also.
Academic librarians are especially likely to have a master's
degree in a subject speciality, in addition to the professional degree in librarianship. One stated that by taking
courses on the same campus where she worked she learned
some of the teachers' interests and was therefore able to
refer people to them. A librarian who had taken a legal
bibliography course at a nearby research library said, "I
got to know the people there, and I know the collection,
and they've all been very helpful."

Training and on-the-job experience are not the only
experiences that give librarians knowledge of outside resources. The librarian who seemed to be the most skilled
and knowledgeable referer had lived in a large city and
makes good use of her familiarity with that city's libraries.
Three other librarians mentioned referrals to libraries in the
towns where they lived or live, and several more mentioned
libraries they had visited for their own use.

In summary, in terms of equity the issue of training contrasts with the consternation cited earlier regarding directors who intervene too much in reference and in referral activities. No librarian complained of receiving too much guidance in general service policy or instruction in specific tools and referral possibilities. Several librarians said they wished they had received more training. Close, tactful observation of and instruction to new staff members, visits to neighboring libraries, workshops, and staff meetings were helpful and appreciated, where employed. Previous and current experience and course work were also described as affecting referral actions.

Two groups whose interests were sometimes overlooked were nonprofessional employees and users. Nonprofessionals are especially subject to being left with reference responsibilities but with very little guidance. Many users are not familiar with the concept of referral, and thus do not complain when it is not offered. Because of this lack of public pressure referral receives little emphasis, with the result that users continue to be uninformed about its possibilities.

Activity Level at Reference Desk

The most plaintive reports of how being overly busy would affect the use of referral came from public librarians. Said one: "Sometimes you're so busy you start looking at the person's stomach and you can't remember which person it was." This individual's supervisor said that, due to cutbacks in staffing, "we just sort of string ourselves along, and often do very superficial reference work." At another site a public librarian described how on a summer day he "could spend an hour with someone because there's enough time to do it." However, during the school year, "if they get three minutes, that's about it, because then there would be a line of people waiting for help." A public research library's subject specialist who stated that he had at times spent an entire day working on one question was an exception.

An academic librarian observed that sometimes there was a "whole class wandering in at once, all asking the same question." Asked if there was always enough time for an adequate response, he replied: "Sometimes you can't answer. Although the class usually will all be doing related stuff,

but then you have other people also who have other questions."

The affect on referral of being very busy varies.
One librarian thought that there was not much relationship
because referral "doesn't take that much time usually," but
someone else stated:

> If a difficult request comes in ... during the day
> when there is good staffing, when I or someone else
> could devote sufficient time to it, it would make a
> difference in the kind of referral that would be done.
> If it comes on an evening or weekend when there's
> only one librarian on duty, that would affect the
> kind of service.

Actually both situations are likely to apply. If the place to
which a referral should be made is obvious, it can be done
quickly. At other times just figuring out which person or
place should be referred to will be a lengthy process.

Finally, there is the referral made because of a lack
of time, cited in one academic library that did not staff its
reference desk at night. There a librarian said that it was
often busy as the time approached for the desk to close, so
that she "may have to refer somebody unnecessarily."

In summary, the data generally seem to indicate that
the librarian who is overwhelmed with requests may make a
less accurate or less complete referral. In some circumstances a referral may be made simply because the librarian
does not have adequate time to handle the question, which
raises the equity issue of overburdening the library referred
to.

Strength of Collection

Surely, a major determinant of the need to make referrals is the strength of the library's collection. The only
library described in an interview as hardly ever needing to
make a referral was a large, specialized one said to have
"the wherewithal to answer anything" in its speciality, and
to rarely receive a question not in its subject area. Elsewhere, however, even strong collections could be unable to
fill a need due to mis-shelving, theft, non-ownership, or
material being in use or at the bindery.

The primary reason libraries cannot purchase all that
their users request is, of course, cost, and librarians spoke
of "drastic" price increases and "mind boggling" funding
requirements. In an academic library several reasons were
cited why a certain subject area might be weak: a new
academic program; a program with a declining enrollment;
or a fringe area, such as nursing on a campus that does
not have a medical school. Sometimes a library's collection
policy is very restricted, such as in an academic library
that did not subscribe to the local newspaper "probably because it's not indexed and not available on microfilm."
Another possibility is that the strength in a collection is
not appropriate to users' needs, as was the case at a public
library where a subject strength had developed because it
was a personal interest of a former director even though,
as one librarian said, "We didn't have a patronage for it."

When a collection is considerably weaker than other
libraries to which referrals have to be made, librarians
sometimes feel frustrated. Interviewees said they were
"embarrassed and a little bit defensive," found the situation
"frustrating," and felt "a little bit like stepchildren." On
the other hand, some librarians did not react this way.
The reference head in a public library said he felt no embarrassment in not owning something because "that's part
of referral--to recognize either that you don't have it or
can't answer it." The director of a small public library
said he now used the lack of resources as an opportunity
to bring attention to inadequate funding, and an academic
librarian said he felt embarrassment if something should be
owned and were not, but he would "quickly pass the buck
to the state" due to inadequate funding.

The reference heads at two of the five academic libraries at which formal interviews were conducted stated
that their users were expected to depend on major research
libraries nearby for specific items. Said one, "The philosophy of the book collection and the reference collection in
here is that students and faculty can do preliminary work
here, even if we do not have the individual monograph that
they need, or the serial that they need, and we have a very
good ... reference collection." The other supervisor stated:

> We really are heavily dependent on referral. My
> boss has said we are a reference library, not a

research library. Our circulating collection is medi-
ocre; we have a pretty good reference collection....
For a term paper on any subject generally we would
have to refer.

In summary, few libraries appear to be so self-
sufficient that referral and requests to other libraries are
only of minor importance, and many have weaknesses in
their collections that make them heavily dependent on other
libraries, at least in some subject areas. For some librarians, frequently having to refer to other libraries causes
feelings of frustration and even embarrassment. Others
seem to be comfortable with the idea that they should rely
on other collections. Still others are unhappy with their
collections' failings, but quickly put the blame on inequitable
funding. This potential inequity to some extent affects both
the librarians and their users, and perhaps the institutions
on which they feel overly dependent.

Availability and Use of Referral Tools

Unless a librarian makes a certain specific referral
often, some type of directory will probably have to be consulted. These include tools available to anyone, such as
local telephone directories; directories usually not owned
by the general public, such as the Encyclopedia of Associations (1985) and the Directory of Special Library and Information Centers (1983); directories created for libraries in
the area, such as union periodical lists; and devices made
for use only in the library in which they are created, such
as card files.

Various referral tools generally were described by librarians as being helpful in referral, but the directory for
one area's network was said to be not "worth much" since
"one public library is supposed to specialize in art, but has
an art budget of $300 a year." In two other libraries the
absence of brochures or directories describing area collections seemed to be a disadvantage. One librarian said that
the local federation had no brochure, and she herself did
not always think to make referrals by going to the reference
office to check a list of libraries and their telephone numbers. In another library, in which the purchase of an expensive microfiche collection was being considered, an interviewee agreed that "it would be useful to know where these

collections are" when advised that this particular collection
was already owned by a nearby library. Newsletters from
local governments, museums, and so on, were also mentioned as containing useful information for making referrals.

Probably the most common and useful referral aids
produced by individual libraries were reported to be card
files. The file may be exclusively for referral, or it may
include other information such as, in one librarian's words,
"things we get asked for a lot; things we have a terrible
time finding, that we found in some obscure book, that might
never be found again." Referral sources listed in such files
were reported to range from service organizations to a local
bird expert. In two libraries, documents librarians had
card files to which they alone had access. This may be
viewed as a reasonable precaution to keep someone not expert in documents from making inaccurate or unnecessary
referrals, but it could also be an example of not sharing
one's personal storehouse of information and therefore inequitable.

Other referral aids described during interviews included mimeographed lists of specialist bookstores and a library's own directory of local services. Some devices refer
the user to other parts of the same institution. These include campus maps; a file of translators on campus; and a
large public library's calendar of events, which pinpoints
events at various branches.

Despite the widespread use of reference and referral
tools, there were a number of indications that more was
needed in this area. The head of reference in one library
not having a file stated, "We probably should develop something but we never have." She agreed that a lot of information was being carried in people's heads, adding, "and at
some point people's heads may leave." The reference chief
in a second library said that there should be a file to include knowledge such as the best local contact for census
information, which "maybe two of us know." A third li-
bary's reference head, who was personally very knowledgeable about other libraries, agreed that a directory of library
collections would be useful: "I can see what you mean. We
sort of know, and for instance we make contacts."

In a fourth library, less interest was expressed. The

reference head said of a card file: "I tried doing that once,
but I never got around to keeping it up." In the same library a reference librarian stated: "This is an undergraduate school, and most people are taking a fairly cut and dried
program, and these things don't come up much."

Nationally published directories do not require an expenditure of in-house or local library association effort for
their maintenance. One such directory said to receive frequent use at some libraries is the Encyclopedia of Associations (1985), which some librarians seem to consider an ex-
cellent alternative to telephoning or referring to a backup
library. When no answer was found in the library, the user
was told to call or write an association dedicated to the topic.
One public librarian declared: "The Encyclopedia of Associations is so wonderful. We use it over and over again
every day." Although this approach saves time involved in
calling a backup library and creates a feeling of not being
overly dependent on another library, there is a problem in
that the association referred to may not have the desired
information or that the answer may be more conveniently
located at a nearby backup library.

In summary, for a library to have useful referral aids,
several things seemed to be necessary. There must be an
interest in referral and an awareness that an organized tool,
such as a card file, will be more useful than a random or
more personalized approach. Time is required to prepare
the directory, map, or other tool if it needs to be created
in-house. A spirit of cooperation, so that files are available to the reference librarian on duty, would seem to be
preferable to files being kept by librarians for their individual use only. Finally, the convenience to the librarian
of making referrals to distant organizations listed in a published directory should be weighed against the convenience
to the user of being offered a closer source. Overall, a
commitment to efficient services, and an equitable position
that not only should local resources be shared, but aids to
sharing those resources should be shared, were perceived
to be required.

Summary of Factors Concerning the
Potential Referrer's Library

Librarians did not often report their directors to be

personally involved in promoting referral, and when directors were involved they sometimes gave more direction than
librarians considered reasonable. Relations with coworkers
seemed to be friendly in most instances, facilitating the exchange of information regarding referral possibilities. Training was generally welcomed but often insufficient, especially
for clerical staff who were expected to assist users when a
librarian was not available. Referral may also suffer if
there is unsufficient staff at the reference desk during a
busy period or if there are inadequate reference tools such
as card files. Weaknesses in library collections, of course,
give rise to referral.

In terms of personal qualities, interpersonal dealings
were aided by tact, and empathy may exist among coworkers. Librarians considered making reasonable demands on
coworkers and providing a reasonable level of work output
to be equitable. Independence from too close supervision
by the director was desired, although conflict may be difficult to avoid given the director's ideas regarding what level
of service is efficient and equitable. Insufficiencies in one's
own library's collection may be felt to be unfair or a reasonable distribution of resources. A lack of needed training
and of referral aids suggests inefficiency, shortage of time,
or that referral has a low priority.

Factors Concerning Outside Resources

From the previous section it appears that the director
is often a remote figure in the referral process. Coworkers,
training, and referral directories can assist the librarian in
making referrals, but even in their absence referrals are
likely to take place. The central need is for the librarian
to know of outside resources that are able to offer assistance.
A minimum level of receptivity between organizations is also
necessary. These considerations will be discussed next.

Strength and Knowledge of Outside Resources

Interviews about referral quite naturally involved discussion about places with which librarians were familiar.
The reason a resource is known is covered under other
topics, such as the already discussed training and experience, and referral tools, and the later treatment of personal

contacts. This factor focuses on the broad diversity of
possible points of referral about which interviewees were
conversant, and also notes one area in which knowledge appeared to be weak, that of United States depository documents.

Public libraries were said to vary greatly in collection
strength. A small one in a rural area was described as being "like a reading club," open only a few hours a day and
not catering "at all" to students. Another small public library was likely to be called by other libraries only when
the question concerned local history. A third small library
gave no information or referral regarding a question on local
history, as a librarian in another state recounted:

> Usually you don't get a "no" and silence. Usually
> you expect to get one idea from the librarian. I
> know I don't feel like I've succeeded if I don't find
> the answer or give somebody an avenue. I got a
> simple "no" from her, and I thought, "That's no
> help."

To an academic librarian, the local public library may mean
no more than a place to refer to when a copy of a popular
magazine is missing. The words "public library," in fact,
seemed to connote to some academic librarians a smaller,
less interesting collection.

Yet, even a small public library branch will receive
referrals if a special strength is known at a library that
does a lot of referring. One busy central library had most
of its articles on a certain subject stolen, so it referred
people to a particular branch library that did not circulate
its periodicals. Stronger, small to medium-sized public libraries can be important points of referral for smaller
branch libraries and smaller libraries in neighboring communities, without attracting many referrals from academic
libraries, it was noted. College students may visit them,
even though such visits were described as being often futile
when the search is for more specialized material. Some
medium-sized public libraries have special strengths, such
as a business collection, which will be objects of referral
by all types of libraries. The larger the public library, the
more likely it may be that the personal knowledge of one
of its librarians will assist in answering a question. As one

interviewee related, when the meaning of two Japanese
terms could not be found in Japanese dictionaries, a large
public library was phoned. It "couldn't find the answer,
but somebody on the staff said there's a large Japanese
population in [town], which nobody on the staff here knew,
and the [town] library was able to answer our question."
The largest public libraries can have strengths in a number
of areas, usually in collections dating back many decades.

A national resource such as New York Public Library's
main research building on Fifth Avenue is in a class by itself. Said one admiring academic librarian:

> I think their librarians are very impressive. They're
> all very scholarly, middle-aged men, not like us who
> are generalists. [They are] old school, not the in-
> formation specialists zipping around with computers.
> They just know how to hit those books--methodical.
> I wouldn't want to live like that, but I respect it.

The characterization may not be entirely accurate since
another librarian remembered calling the library with a reference question and receiving the benefit of an instantaneous
computer search. Even this major library received criticisms, with complaints being voiced about a vastness that
confuses users, high photocopying fees, difficulty in getting
through by telephone, and waiting for a long time in the
reading room for books to be retrieved.

As regards academic libraries, two-year college libraries received little mention as sites for referral. A
four-year college, however, usually had something to recom-
mend it for referrals, whether it be due to a collection relating to the school's religious affiliation, documents depository status, former role as a teacher's college, or some other
feature. An academic library may be referred to for night
or Sunday use when a public library is closed, and one
public librarian said she referred to a nearby college library
for a public typewriter when her own library's typewriter
was not working. Medical and law libraries, and large academic libraries, draw referrals for their impressive collections. As one public librarian stated:

> If they want something really obscure, like say they
> wanted a newspaper from a foreign country and I

> know the colleges probably won't have it--well, I
> know [college] has a few European newspapers--but
> if it's something that sounds like really far out, I
> would say, "Well, you can try [university] because
> they have so much."

Librarians in a large university system are likely to make
the majority of their referrals to libraries within the same
system.

Librarians in smaller academic libraries claimed that
some of the appeal of the big university libraries is unjusti-
fied. Students were said to often go to the biggest libraries
for the same material that was available in their own school's
library. Students even went to a large university library
for subjects not in that institution's curriculum, and in
which their own library was stronger. One librarian in a
moderate-sized academic library said that students of a
large university used his library, however, because it was
a "nice, integrated collection" in which they did not feel
lost.

Often the user may think of an appropriate public or
academic library to try once his or her own library proves
not to have the needed item, but users are less likely to
know of special libraries to which they may turn. Trying
a library specializing in the area of need can be a gratify-
ing experience. One librarian told how she had been unable to find out the name of the creator of a particular
painting from her usual backup library for such questions.
Finally she phoned the library at the Metropolitan Museum
of Art, from where she was referred to the European painting division. As a result: "Before I had the sentence
finished she gave me the answer. I loved that. She was
so good." Occasionally libraries contacted the Library of
Congress or the National Library of Medicine. State libraries were turned to for legislative information. Other
sources mentioned were company libraries for scientific journals, a veterans' hospital for medical journals, a Federal
Archives and Records Center for genealogy, a state agency
for reasonably priced computerized bibliographic searching,
a local historical society for genealogy, and a courthouse
library for legal material.

During the interviewing it was generally assumed that

most referrals were made to libraries. A reference supervisor at one large public library said, however, that most
of her referrals might not be to libraries. One of the many
types of places contacted were foreign consulates, as in
requesting a copy of a talk in Hungarian. In another public library an interviewee said a user had called her back to
thank her for suggesting he try a travel agency to obtain
a copy of the calendar of the Ontario Shakespeare Festival.
"It's such an ad hoc process," she commented. An academic
librarian found a local newspaper morgue helpful.

     In one area librarians were noticeably weak in their
knowledge of outside resources, that of United States documents depository collections. Interviewees were not quizzed
on the full range of their knowledge of specific referral
possibilities, but misunderstandings regarding depository
services were obvious. For example, the knowledgeable
and well organized reference head at one public library did
not know that a nearby large library having many depository
documents was obligated by law to admit the public. The
reference head in an academic library did not know that a
nearby library to which frequent referrals were made was a
depository, although this is partially explained by the fact
that there were other larger depositories nearby. An interviewee in a public library said of a nearby depository,
"They're a depository so I just assume they have everything," not realizing that only a few depository libraries
choose to receive all documents available for distribution.
One of her coworkers did not bother to furnish users with
the Superintendent of Documents classification numbers by
which the nearby depository arranged its documents, even
though these numbers appear in the Publications Reference
File (U.S. Government Printing Office), which her library
used to identify documents. She assumed, incorrectly, that
the depository had a card catalog of its documents arranged
by title. A documents librarian complained, "Often people
are referred to us without a prior phone call. People will
come twenty miles and wonder why we don't have a specific
document."

     Even documents librarians had gaps in their knowledge.
An academic librarian thought that a depository in a nearby
state was a regional depository, which would mean it received
all depository documents titles, but it was neither a regional
nor a selective depository choosing to receive all available

documents, and thus should not have been referred to for
some items. Nor could documents librarians always count
on their coworkers to make necessary referrals to them.
In a large public library housing a depository, a reference
librarian said that there were "not too many" referrals to
the documents collection because "I think people are just
not aware of what is available with U.S. documents. Plus
it is difficult. I think it is very difficult to locate things."

In summary, a wide range of library and non-library
resources are used by librarians as sites to which referrals
can be made. Most types of libraries were reported to receive referrals, although two year college and small public
libraries received relatively few. The larger a library is,
the more referrals it is likely to receive, but this generalization must be tempered by such factors as their being
thought to be too confusing for some users. In addition,
some librarians make a large percentage of referrals to non-
library agencies. As for Government documents referrals,
examples were cited of librarians not knowing where depositories were, what proportion of documents available for
distribution nearby depositories received, what depositories'
obligations towards the public were, or what use was made
of Superintendent of Documents numbers.

Nonpersonal Relations with Outside Resources

A key consideration in referral is the reception expected from the place to which a referral is made. Will the
referring librarian or the user being referred be rejected
or given insufficient assistance? Under this topic situations
will be described according to whether the points of referral
were perceived to be helpful, ambiguous, or unhelpful. All
these relations are classified as nonpersonal to distinguish
them from the following topic, that of personal contacts.

Helpful outside resources. A minimum level of coop-
erativeness is largely guaranteed in formal library networks,
through which libraries are obligated to help each other.
Such arrangements affect smaller public libraries the most.
As one librarian said of her experience working in such a
library, "Referral was easy--to the area library." A reference head at a smaller public library mentioned "deliberately
going out of the library network without a reason" as an
example of "bad" referral. At another small public library,

hesitant to make a request by phone. An academic librarian
stated:

> Well, if I called up with a reference question I would
> feel it had to be in terms of: "Hi, I'm having a
> problem. I was hoping you could help me. Do you
> know anything about such and such?" I'd identify
> myself as a librarian. It's like conferring. I'm
> asking them for advice. I'm really not asking them
> to do the work for me.

The interviewee who appeared to have the deepest reluctance
to telephone said, "Maybe I don't do it because I feel I'm
imposing on another person on the other end, but on the
other hand [nearby academic library] does call us." This
librarian seemed to feel inferior even though the other library was similar to his own. Such an attitude would limit
calling either to obtain an answer or to arrange the referral
of a user.

     What has been discussed so far has several equity im-
plications. Some libraries receive money to serve as backup
libraries, so at least some referrals by libraries they are
supposed to serve are justified. Some libraries extend
service to outsiders even though they are not obligated to
do so, although there may often be a sense of earning the
right to receive favors in return. Referring librarians are
often conscious of a need to not make unnecessary demands
on either the reimbursed or the nonreimbursed libraries,
especially if it will be known that the request or referral
came from their library.

     The closeness with which libraries can work with each
other without entering into a formal agreement can be seen
in collection sharing, often a basis for referral. The reference head at one of two neighboring academic libraries reported that some meetings had taken place between the staff
of the two libraries, noting "I can't say we're sharing, but
at least we're communicating knowledge so that if they're
dropping something we probably wouldn't want to drop it
the same year." She said that there was no formal agreement for fear that the governing boards of each institution
would make a conclusion such as: "Oh, you've been using
[college] for that. Okay, we don't need this. We don't
need the library. Our students can use that." Also cited

as an example of collection sharing, by a public library reference head, was his practice of sending a list of his library's periodicals to "all the special libraries in the county," which in turn often provided copies of their lists.

Finally, the mere guarantee of a positive reception does not mean necessarily that referrals will be made. There were examples among the librarians interviewed of ones who made frequent referrals within a library consortium of which their library was a member, and ones who made infrequent use of a consortium because they did not believe referrals were necessary or because they considered the resources of the other consortium members to be inadequate.

Ambiguous outside resources. Before the focus turns to the negative view, that of unhelpful library relations, examples will be given of in-between situations, in which libraries are perceived as helpful or unhelpful depending on the attitude of the librarian encountered. The head of reference in a public library serving as an area backup complained regarding a more specialized backup library that there was "one dame at the desk who could not give a hot hoot in hell whether you ask a question of her or not." One of his subordinates remembered someone saying that the specialized library never answers a question, but "I shouldn't even mention it because one person said it." An interviewee in another public library stated that the specialized library had always been helpful. These different impressions indicate how variable and how vulnerable a library's reputation can be.

Other problems cited with backup libraries included one in which the reference desk was sometimes staffed by someone with little familiarity with reference work, such as a cataloger; and another in which the person taking telephone requests was not tactful. Describing the latter case, a reference supervisor stated:

> There was a time when I was in here when people were reluctant to refer to [backup library] because the person they were calling would given them a hard time on their interview, and she was right.... They weren't getting the information from the interview, or they weren't looking up all the sources, but she was intimidating people by the way she did it.

More ambiguous for referring librarians is a situation
in which a library's policy restricting use by outsiders is
applied unequally, or is not strictly applied. A reference
head at an academic library said, "I make a point of steering students away from law schools because they do not
want undergraduate students." Another interviewee in the
same library indicated that he did not make referrals to
nearby law school libraries because of their "fairly restrictive" policies regarding outsiders, noting "We have a letter
about their policy. I don't know it off hand." Yet a public
library reference head in the same town said that the same
law school library was "very helpful," and she referred
there often. Regarding a county law library that the other
library relied on, she observed: "They primarily only allow
students of law in. They have very short hours, so it's
hard to get to them..., and I don't find them that helpful
always."

Also confusing is when a library's policy vacilates.
A public librarian said that a small medical library currently
lacked staff to help users, and that there was a "big security problem" in the building, so that "sometimes they don't
want to let people in who don't have credentials or are just
saying, 'I want to go in and use the library.'" As a result,
"We get different responses as to whether they'll help a patron or not."

Unhelpful outside resources. By "unhelpful" is meant
restrictions on use by outsiders beyond those applied by
nearly all libraries. Thus not extending direct borrowing
privileges to outsiders is not unhelpful in this sense since
most libraries would require that interlibrary loan procedures
be followed unless there is a cooperative borrowing arrangement. Denying in-person access is unhelpful. "Unhelpful"
can also refer to service that is rendered, but in a grudg-
ing manner.

Restrictions are more common at special libraries and
private academic libraries, least common at public libraries.
One company librarian noted that scientists are not welcome
in other companies' libraries. Sometimes a company librarian
must be equally careful about asking assistance from outsiders. For example, a librarian who had worked at a publishing firm's library said that if the firm were considering
diversifying into another area, she would be warned,
"Look, this is secret."

Restrictions on access are found at all sizes of private academic libraries, but it is the largest ones with the much valued collections that receive the most attention because of their policies. One such institution was severely criticized in two different libraries. A law librarian said that it was "her only problem." "They don't help over the 'phone, and I once sent a student there who was turned away," she remarked, adding that the librarian there had been "very uncooperative and nasty." In another academic library the reference supervisor said that librarians at this university would "sneer" when she telephoned them, and that she had to identify her library as a member of a consortium "before they'll even talk to me." Omission of small bits of information in making referrals through the consortium had brought complaining letters to her director. Furthermore, she stated, "They're even nasty when you go there."

Restrictions on use were not always spoken of disapprovingly at other libraries, however, and librarians in the same library can disagree about how much demand should be placed on a private academic library. One academic reference supervisor said candidly:

> I consider it's my job to provide information to my users by any means possible. I'm more concerned about my users being able to get what they need than I am about [private academic library] having one more person roaming through their stacks. I mean, anybody I send there I'm assuming to be a responsible person that will make proper use of the collection.

Thus, she argued that her first responsibility is to her own users, and that she sends only responsible people. She then made three further arguments:

> I never send anybody out until I've checked my own collection first; but, I think, given that, the number of people they're receiving from me is not that terrific as to place an undue strain on their collection, and I think the people should be treated with courtesy. I make no distinction between people in [her college] and people from outside.

She now has made the additional points that she does not

refer unnecessarily, she does not refer too many people, and she herself does not discriminate against outsiders. There is yet another justification: "We don't have enough [subject area] journals. People are always marching in here and saying, 'I want to go to [private academic library].'" Her users, then, are clamoring for access permits to this particular research library.

Even with the marshalling of all these arguments, she cannot fully suppress her feelings of behaving inequitably. "We really take advantage--a net borrower rather than a net lender," she stated, admitting: "I guess it's hard for me being from a small library to relate to the terrible problems of a research library."

This librarian's coworkers claimed that they first tried to make referrals to a less convenient public research library. One said he explained to users that the more desired library is private. The other said that she only used the private library "in desperation" because that was consortium policy and because the private library was "busy enough with their own."

Additional arguments made by interviewees against restrictions on access to large private academic libraries include that they receive large amounts of public funding and that claims of theft by outsiders rather than by the institution's own students are not documented. It was pointed out that a possible compromise is to have restricted access only "for certain times of the week when staffing isn't as great."

Publicly supported academic libraries usually do not restrict in-library use, although one such library was said to have adopted restrictions because of security problems. In one regard both publicly supported and private academic libraries were found to be less cooperative than public libraries: They were less likely to check the shelf for callers to see if a book were in.

Despite their generally less restrictive policies, public libraries can also be unfriendly, as described in the previous section on ambiguous libraries. Other examples were a large city library where it was said staff "can be very snippy," and the complaint of a reference head in a small public

library that her backup library refused to forward a question to a research library. The director of a small public
library said that libraries in the area had not joined a local
federation "because they see it as competition." A librarian
in a backup public library said that personnel at the next
largest public library in the area "don't particularly like to
have to refer to us, at least that's what I've been told,
that they would prefer to be the area library and therefore
don't like coming to us if they can help it, although they
do." Local public agencies can also be unfriendly, as seen
in the one complaint that one "can't even get annual reports
from City Hall."

Much may depend on personalities. A public reference
head, asked if another public library did not like to lend or
borrow from other libraries because it felt it was protecting
a superior collection, answered in the negative, adding, "I
think it depends on the people in the libraries." She suggested that "maybe in some cases people would rather not
establish that relationship with other libraries, would rather
just be insular, and use their own collections." Similarly,
an academic reference head said of library systems, "Sometimes they work well and sometimes they don't, a lot of times
because of the personality of the staff."

Own policy towards outsiders. Closely related to the
issue of referral to outsiders is that of a library's policy
regarding serving outsiders. Such users may have been
referred or may have decided on their own to attempt to
use the library. While there were few admissions of taking
unfair advantage of outside resources, there were also few
indications that librarians interviewed were willing to assist
outsiders simply from kindness. In both situations the in-
tent seemed to be to seek a balance in exchange, even if
unequal resources made this impossible to achieve entirely.

An example of expecting to gain in return for generous
actions is the unilateral extension of borrowing privileges
to outside people, meaning those whom the library does not
primarily exist to serve. An academic librarian said that
courtesy cards for borrowing books were given to all visiting
professors "partially" as a "PR [public relations] thing."
A librarian at another academic library that extended generous borrowing privileges said that "the college president
feels it's extremely important for public relations." An

academic library director, however, said that he had seen the issuance of courtesy cards fail as a way to raise money from alumni and therefore he was no longer issuing such cards.

Helping another library's clientele also means expecting assistance for one's own users in return. An academic librarian said that one reason borrowing privileges were extended to local businesses was that the library liked "to be on good terms with chemical companies because we're not a strong science library and we have a fair number of science majors here."

Librarians reported not wanting to feel too much in debt. Said one academic reference head about a county college library that called with requests but to which few referrals were made: "This is my philosophy: We're only a small collection, and it's very nice to have somebody who needs us, as well as our needing somebody else." One of this person's subordinates stated:

> We are very comfortable with [college library] because they call us more than we call them. We try to build good will, and my assumption is if we don't overextend our welcome then it will be maintained at equilibrium.

An academic reference supervisor in a small library that belonged to a consortium providing access to major research libraries admitted that she was dependent on the larger libraries, but she noted that she was also generous in that she had provided outsiders with "little" free computer searches.

Legal obligation was another reason for helping outsiders. In two academic libraries, documents librarians mentioned that they gave more complete service when answering documents questions because of the duty of a depository to serve the public. The head of a reference desk at a large backup library said that she sometimes felt her library's local users were slighted because long distance calls were more likely to be made for questions phoned in from other libraries since state funding was received for this purpose.

There was just one librarian who appeared to be acting

inequitably but feeling no remorse. She and her coworkers admitted that the library to which they made the most referrals was perhaps a certain private academic library, yet she stated that if students from that college asked her "for a lot of assistance, I might refer them back to their own institution." This librarian's ungenerous attitude was apparently motivated by her anger at what she saw as too many demands made on her library by outsiders. She stated, "We can't be magnanimous and stretch ourselves to the people who aren't paying for us now because we're really running ragged for what we've got, trying to maintain the quality of what we've got." Two of this person's coworkers also complained of overuse by outsiders, and in this atmosphere the statement of a younger librarian who had been on the staff less than a year seemed startling: "That's the whole reason for us being here, as far as I can see it. Help as many people as you can." Such a statement can be viewed as either highly principled or as naive.

Annoyance at excessive use by outside people was also expressed by a law librarian, who complained that service was owed "basically to students and faculty, but somewhere things got turned around because we seem to be helping attorneys much more." Considerable annoyance was also expressed at excessive interlibrary loan requests. Some librarians reported that having their holdings listed in the OCLC (Online Computer Library Center) network had resulted in their receiving large numbers of such requests. One reference head stated:

> We do a lot, and it's expensive. You sit down and figure out how much each item costs you, and it's horrifying. You figure manpower, and xeroxing, and postage, and all the time that's involved in processing it, filling out the forms. It comes to a lot of money.

With so many librarians recently linked by OCLC, a sort of psychological bartering system is emerging. An academic librarian stated that the library's interlibrary loan librarian kept track of whom loans were "owed" to, and would say: "Oh boy! This is the first request from this library."

Very few librarians interviewed worked where both in-person access and telephone reference assistance to outsiders were restricted, as is more common in large private academic research libraries. Academic librarians in general did not do as much phone reference for outsiders, but they were also less inclined to do it for their primary clientele. Where restrictions did exist, they were not always enforced. At an academic library with restricted in-person and telephone access, an interviewee said callers were asked "if they're our own faculty, or students, or alumni, but if somebody just asks a quick question I'll probably get an answer." A public librarian who contended that local residents "are entitled to all the help you can give them," but nonresidents are "not entitled to any help whatsoever," still found time eventually to answer letters from out of state seeking genealogical information.

To summarize the entire discussion of nonpersonal relations with outside resources, the respondent librarians reported that they can usually count on courteous assistance when referring a user or otherwise seeking assistance from another institution. Some libraries with no legal obligations to serve outsiders were said to be especially generous. Instances in which a librarian telephoned for help was discourteous were usually ascribed to the "orneriness" of a particular librarian, although there is one major academic library from which such responses were said to be standard.

Whether dealing with a generous library or one not eager to serve outsiders, librarians claimed to be careful to not make unnecessary demands. The most sensitive issue seemed to be in-person use of large private academic libraries. Librarians marshalled arguments as to why they should be able to direct users to them for in-person access, but at the same time expressed guilt for adding to the load of what they realized might be severely overburdened institutions.

Making unnecessary requests is inequitable, but is breaking network rules? Some librarians thought that rules established so that unfair demands were not made on some libraries could be justifiably ignored if they interfered with providing the best service to the user. Other librarians thought such rule breaking was a serious offense, although it is not certain what they would have thought if they had not been satisfied with the service provided by the formal network.

The comment by one reference supervisor that cooperation in collection building with another nearby library
must be kept informal so that governing boards would not
see it as an excuse to reduce funding raises other issues of
equity and ethics. Trying to make one's library appear to
be more in need than it actually is may be the common thing
to do, but is it the right thing to do?

Closely related to referring is assisting outsiders.
There was a noticeable lack of expression of feelings of
kindness or generosity in such service. Generally it was
said to be done as part of an informal system of reciprocity,
or at least for "public relations" value.

Restrictions safeguard against being overused, but
they can result in a library receiving more help than it
provides to outsiders. No librarian expressed concern that
her or his institution's were unwarranted. The bending of
restrictions that took place may have been an admission,
however, that unless all libraries are equally restrictive,
barriers meant to correct an inequitable overuse of one's
own resources can create an imbalance in the other direction.

Extent of Personal Contacts

When people need help, they are likely to turn to individuals with whom they are on cordial terms rather than
to strangers. These individuals may be described as "personal contacts" or more specifically as "friends" or "acquaintances" depending on how close the relationship is.
Thus librarians call on their friends and acquaintances outside their own library when making referrals. Questions
addressed here include how beneficial such contacts are and
ways in which they are made.

Librarians interviewed spoke of being traditionally
helpful to one another, but there was also expression of
appreciation for the extra effort sometimes felt to be owed
to someone known personally. This extra effort is not only
due to friendliness but also, as one librarian stated, to the
trust the outside contact has that the referring librarian is
making a "bona fide referral" deserving of assistance.

At times friendships between librarians result in their
acting as couriers to speed the delivery of material to their

users. Rather than waiting for a loan item to make its way
through regular channels, two library directors made exchanges when meeting for lunch. Two other librarians
working in the same area and living near each other stopped
by each other's house with interlibrary loan deliveries.
Such efforts must arise not only from belief in what to expect from a friend, but also from a strong sense that users
are worthy of such consideration.

Sometimes friendship and efficiency are in conflict.
A reference head made frequent referrals for a particular
subject to a library in which he had a friend. Another
supervisor (who joined in the conversation briefly) said she
would refer to another library only about a fifth as far away
for the same subject, whereupon the reference head said he
had forgotten that library and it was indeed the best place
to refer to. As one librarian stated, "Personal contacts
make it easier ... to remember the possibilities," but they
also can cause one to forget more efficient options.

Some ways of forming contacts take less effort and
therefore can be considered more efficient than others. The
easiest are the ones that arise naturally from having once
been employed by a library or having former library school
classmates working in the area. In a related case the "only
reason" a librarian referred to a certain department of one
library was that it used to be headed by a former coworker's
husband. In another setting a former coworker was consulted by telephone because of her highly regarded expertise. In general, reference heads, whom one would expect
to have had more opportunities to make contacts, did in fact
report having more contacts.

Attending local meetings is important in fulfilling three
different purposes: hearing new information, making contacts, and inspecting the collection of the library in which
the meeting is being held. Two reference chiefs mentioned
joining the Special Libraries Association as a way to make
useful contacts. The Exemplary Referrer stated that through
a contact made in this association students were now permitted to use a nearby company library.

Telephoning a library a number of times and thereby
becoming familiar with its staff can make it easier to telephone it than a less familiar library. An interlibrary loan

librarian commented regarding her counterpart at a backup
library:

> I keep saying one of us will go into bends if we
> don't talk to the other one every day. You know,
> we have to have these conversations constantly, but
> we were talking who knows about what. We go from
> subject to subject before we could finish.

Interviewees also spoke of becoming "garrulous" and "very
friendly" on the telephone with librarians they had never
met face to face.

Asking for a particular librarian by name when telephoning is sometimes necessary, but at times is objected to
by librarians on three grounds: causing delay in obtaining
information (violating efficiency), overburdening the librarian
being sought (violating equity), and being unfair to the librarians passed over (also violating equity). An interlibrary
loan librarian who invited calls for ILL requests discovered
that "what happens is that if they've got any kind of question, they've got my name, so they'll call."

There was at least one type of contact that was rejected. An art appraiser approached a librarian about obtaining referrals in return for some as yet unspecified reimbursement. The librarian turned down the offer because it
"would have violated ethics." Another example of a contact
viewed as either not achievable or not worth pursuing was
cited by a children's librarian, a former school librarian,
who said that she did not see how she could interact with
the local school librarians because they were Parent-Teacher
Association mothers possessing "no standing in the school."

Another hindrance to making contacts may operate
when a local association formed to encourage library cooperation is likely to have only a few designated representa-
tives from each library, so that other staff members are excluded. Library positions specifically designed for interaction
with other libraries, such as that of interlibrary loan librarian, are the ones that are more likely to provide an opportunity to attend meetings of libraries in a local area.
This is efficient in a sense, but limits the number of librarians likely to make contacts and thereby potentially able to
better refer users. Formal visits to allow staff to become

familiar with other libraries may be considered to be too
time consuming. Said one librarian:

> We made more visits to other libraries when I first
> started working here, and that was nice. It made
> it a lot easier to call. You knew what you were
> likely to find at the other end and what the re-
> sponse was likely to be, but we don't have time
> now.

It is possible then for the efficiency considerations of
limited time and limited staff to interfere with the formation
of contacts, leaving the relationship with outside librarians
more often that of stranger to stranger. Within these impersonal relationships one library can still make considerable, indirect demands on another. Thus a public librarian
said that she "couldn't really say" if there were a good relationship between her library and a nearby academic library
to which the most referrals for in-person use were made because she did not "do that much with them on the phone."
In other words, because she referred to this library but
neither telephoned it nor met with its librarians, she did
not know if her referrals were welcomed or resented.

In summary the respondents clearly indicated how
personal contacts can make a significant contribution to reference and referral service. Through them librarians know
whom to contact for specific types of information, receive
especially thorough service, and sometimes personally de-
liver needed material. They also create inefficiency, such
as when users are referred to a more distant library than
necessary because of having a personal contact there, or
when librarians spend too much time in friendly conversation.

Personality plays a part in the formation of such contacts, with some librarians becoming very friendly with people they only talk to on the telephone. Opportunity is also
important, so that an interlibrary loan specialist is likely to
have more contacts. Relationships can be fostered by formal
and informal visits, and by attendance at local meetings.

Ties with outsiders can be viewed in equity terms, in
that between friends one both owes and is owed special consideration. Alternatively, it can be argued that the service
rendered is done out of empathic feeling for the friend in

need. The exact motivation is likely to vary with the individual and with the situation.

Interaction with Faculty
(in Academic Libraries)

Academic librarians refer to teaching faculty and are affected by referrals by faculty. A few librarians complained that faculty referred students to other libraries unnecessarily. From an equity viewpoint, their library was being slighted, other libraries were being overtaxed, and the student was being inconvenienced.

Said one librarian of referrals to a nearby prestigious university library:

> Most referrals to [other library] come from faculty who make the assumption that this library does not have the wherewithal, and of course you should go to [other library]. Well, I resent that kind of thing.

Another librarian reported:

> For science materials, I've had students who have asked--their teacher says what they need is at [company library]. That is basically the question, so we would call up and arrange for them to go 'cause [company library] is down the street.

She contended that "the faculty member probably would be having them use the same material we have here." Another similar referral situation mentioned by one person was that of "a lot of part-time adjunct people who I think use their standard reading list and send people to the library to look up a book without checking if we own it."

Referrals to faculty by librarians did not seem to be very frequent, although the only statement opposing such referrals was from someone saying that he would not refer a question from the general public to the faculty because he saw it "as our responsibility, not the faculty's." Most referrals were to faculty members known to librarians by name. As to whether professors welcomed the extra work load, one reference supervisor commented:

I figure that's their job. Also, most people I know
who are working in an area, I would know that because I talked to them, which probably means that
they're pretty easy to talk to.

Another reference head said that "sometimes with honor students when they're trying to pick out a topic and they need
some help in choosing, I suggest that they talk to individuals on the staff, and frankly I have never had anybody who
wasn't willing to do that kind of thing." A subject specialist noted that if "somebody is writing a paper and gets very
enthusiastic, I say, 'Well, you ought to speak to [profes-
sor]; it would be interesting for you,' and the students love
to do that."

A sensitive type of interaction with faculty involves
an unclear assignment, perhaps one that seems to have been
poorly conceived or inadequately explained to the student.
Problems with assignments also confront public librarians,
one of whom regularly sent letters to teachers in cases of
"massive assignments and not enough materials." She received only one or two responses and tried telephoning, but
the teachers never phoned her back. Furthermore, she
stated, "the illogic of some assignments is astonishing."

A college librarian said that sometimes difficulties with
assignments could be avoided by referring the student to
the relevant library subject specialist, who was in close
touch with the professors concerning books put on reserve
and what was expected of the student. In a second library
the reference head said that she referred people back to
their advisors "a lot" to clarify questions. In a third the
following caution was offered:

If a person simply comes to find a correct format
for a bibliographic citation, you can give them the
best format, but that's incorrect. What you should
say is, "What is your teacher's instruction?"

The previously mentioned Exemplary Referrer received
a list of subjects from professors to assist her in giving ori-
entations to freshman classes. Doing an orientation "in a
vacuum," she said, was a "waste of time." Another of her
helpful practices was to ask students the names of their
professors. She explained, "The reason I ask is that some

faculty members have idiosyncracies and you get to know
them, and you know they won't accept things from one journal and they will from another, and you know what style
they're interested in."

Another of her approaches seems particularly produc-
tive and worthy of imitation. She does not tell the student
to re-check an assignment with a professor, but rather calls
the professor herself "because if the assignment isn't clear
to the student the first time, I doubt he's going to get it
clear the second time." Besides getting a "very clear impression of what the faculty member wants," the conversation serves additional purposes:

> I can also say, "You know, we don't have these
> sources," or, "Did you know we have this or that?"
> I'm not argumentative. I do it in a nice way, so
> it's a way of building up rapport with that faculty
> member also, and I try to tactfully explain that they
> could give it to the student on a ditto sheet. It's
> a lot easier than verbally because verbally you'll
> get twenty students, you'll get twenty interpreta-
> tions.

Telephoning faculty, which she tried to get the rest of the
reference staff to do, is "a big problem with co-adjuncts
because they just come and teach the courses and leave,
and I have to track them down, but I don't mind doing
that."

Some interviewees were involved in organized efforts
to relate to faculty. Liaison programs, in which each librarian works with the faculty in a particular subject area,
were, in the words of one librarian, used for "promoting
the library and using some of their information as well as
to strengthen the library." Another person said that the
amount of eye-to-eye contact with each person varied with
the department since "there are some departments that are
definitely individuals, and there are other departments
where it's basically the chair and the department group
consensus." Other outreach techniques mentioned included
a library open house featuring demonstrations of online computerized searching, and distribution of an acquisitions list
or newsletter.

In summary, faculty who refer to other libraries at the expense of an adequate on-campus library are seen as unfair to both libraries and the students. Referring to faculty, while infrequently used except for clarifying assignments, was felt by most librarians to be in accord with the responsibilities of the faculty.

The Exemplary Referrer really shone in regard to checking assignments. Treating the assignment, the professor, and the student with high respect, she telephoned faculty, "tracking them down" if necessary, to clarify the work required, explain resources, and tactfully suggest written instructions as opposed to verbal. Other examples of marketing of services and building referral contacts were liaison programs, open houses, and newsletters or acquisitions lists.

Summary of Factors Concerning Outside Resources

Librarians interviewed made referrals to a broad range of libraries and agencies. Relations with outside resources were usually cordial, but there was considerable sensitivity to the equity consideration of how much service is given to outsiders versus how much is received from outside institutions. Personal contacts in other libraries helped to provide assurance of assistance and an atmosphere less charged with worry over who might be taking advantage of the other. In academic libraries, relations with faculty members were sometimes too remote, and some faculty offended librarians' sense of equity by making unnecessary referrals to other libraries.

Factors Concerning the User

Along with the librarian's knowledge of receptive places to refer to, the referral act requires the librarian to make a judgment regarding a particular user's need for referral. This evaluation can be a complex process, as the following section documents. The skillfulness of the reference interview; the user's demeanor, status, and willingness to travel; and the reputation of urban areas for safety; all play a part. Completing the equation is the possibility of feedback, usually in terms of the user directly advising the librarian of the merit of the referral.

Evaluation of the User

This factor includes both the librarian's skill in conducting a reference interview that ascertains the user's true need, and the librarian's judgment concerning how much help should be given to a particular request. This judgment is of two types: deciding what help is required to meet the user's need and at times, it seems, also judging the user's deservedness.

Librarians vary in interviewing skill. Appearing less adept is the one who confided: "I find it's very difficult to really pinpoint people, what they want, so you kind of have to drop them into the area of what they want, and they'll give you clues as to what they really want."

The most challenging user seems to be the student who displays one or more of the following elements: ignorance, inarticulateness, shyness, and feigned or real indifference. Several experienced academic librarians spoke knowledgeably of how to assist such students. The Exemplary Referrer used humor:

> I'll try to kid them. I'll say, "Are you writing for the CIA?, because if you don't give me all the information I can't help you," and I've learned that what they ask you the first time is not necessarily what they really want, and you have to really dig to find out what they're really after. There's a technique to the reference interview. I never take it at face value.

She analyzed the seemingly disinterested students thus: "Sometimes I find that the students who come poorly prepared, it may be a defense mechanism, that they just don't want to let on that they don't know, and they're defensive, so they pick this nonchalant attitude to cover up an inferiority or a feeling of inferiority."

Another academic librarian described how he reassured students. In the initial encounter he would say: "If you want more information, come back. Don't hesitate." Sometimes the student would return saying, "I'm sorry to bother you again," and he would reply: "You're not bothering me. That is what I'm here for." He concluded that "if you

encourage this, at least a facade that you are interested,
that you don't mind them bothering you, they do come
back." A careless interviewer, one academic reference
head noted, can miss the necessity for a referral:

> I have come across librarians who say to a student,
> "Look here," or, "Look there." They don't work
> with the student, and frequently students have to
> be drawn out. They don't know what they're sup-
> posed to be asking, and that's a long process, and
> it requires then maybe ultimately the person has to
> be referred to someone off of the campus.

Public librarians mentioned users who "say not to call
for them because they think they are bothering us," or who
ask, "Are you sure you want to do that?," when the librarian offers to call another library for them. From an equity
viewpoint, these users appear to feel unworthy of a librarian's attention. Indeed, telephoning for users can be demanding of a librarian's time and also expensive if long-
distance calls are made. An academic librarian said regarding telephoning to locate material, "If it's not busy we'll do
it sometimes, but I have a tendency to let the kid because
I figure they can dial it as easily as I can, and why should
I waste my time on the phone?" A second academic librarian
pointed out that often many students are looking for the
same book so that calling will not succeed in locating a
copy, and a third did not think that even if she did call to
locate a volume that "any library would check the shelf."

Some librarians were under pressure to reduce long-
distance phone bills, although such pressure was occasionally resisted. Said one reference head who had been questioned by the library director about charges for distant
calls, "I will often say an amount of money for reference
use of the phone should be in the budget." A public librarian said that he telephoned for "some people who come
in of really minimal intelligence or who look as though they
don't have the money for another phone call." An academic
librarian stated that he allowed students to use his telephone
to call somewhat distant libraries "so it's never on their
budget."

Obviously some librarians want very much to help users
who are not adept at helping themselves. One public library

reference head said she would tend to do more for someone who "looks completely inept and, you know, helpless in a library situation." Interviewees spoke of trying to overcome their users' fear of being referred to unfamiliar surroundings. A children's librarian told of the care she took to reassure the children she found it necessary to refer to the adult department. Both an academic and a public librarian said that when referring they might overcome users' fear of the unfamiliar by describing physical layouts and telling them that there would be someone there to assist them. Two other librarians said that they assured users that they had the right to use particular libraries considered to be unfriendly to outsiders. Both concern for users' rights and empathy are evident in these various types of assistance.

Some users, students included, are not at all shy about asking for help. In fact, some are too demanding. Librarians complained of students who "just expect everything to be handed to them," and "keep coming back with the same question" even after they have been told that they must do some of the research themselves. A female academic reference head observed that some foreign students, especially Africans and Asians, "come to this country usually from the wealthy class, and they have a caste system in their mind, and they tend to treat librarians like dirt." In another academic library foreign students were also found to exhibit "a certain amount of arrogance," expecting a female librarian to do much of their work for them.

An academic reference head refused to give maximum service to students who did not allow themselves enough time to complete their assignments: "If the student comes to me on a Thursday and the paper is due on Friday, forget it, I will not knock myself out." An academic librarian confessed to becoming angry

> when you suddenly get that glassy look that says, "I don't really know what I'm looking for," and you say, "Are you doing this for somebody else?" And they say, "Yeah, for my boy friend." And I'll make a remark about, "Isn't he bright enough to do it for himself?" You know, I don't like that. Or if I'm not that bitter I'll say, "It's easier for me to be helpful if I speak to the person who wants it directly." That's what I should say, right?

In a similar vein, a public librarian admitted, "I started getting really annoyed at the mothers coming in and wanting you to do their kids' work."

The disinterested student is annoying. Commented an academic librarian:

> We've had people come in and ask for material we don't have. We've called another library and tried to get the information. These people never come back, or when you do find the information ... they couldn't care less.

This librarian also noted that some students do not want to be referred to another library:

> Some of them, once they learn they have to go to another library and travel, maybe spend money on carfare, or take half a day out of their life and go to downtown [city] and ask another librarian to help them out, will just say: "Forget about it. I'll just slap something together I can get here and shovel it in for a grade."

It is hard to blame this librarian for being "not apt to put out as much" for someone who is "lackadaisical," yet he himself admits, "Sometimes I feel guilty about that."

The case of the student who does not seem very dedicated is not as simple as it might at first seem. The most generalizable conclusion from comments regarding students not requiring referral, based on statements from all the academic libraries and several of the public libraries, is that students have a lot of leeway in selecting material for their research papers. Said one librarian:

> On a college campus you have a relative necessity of getting a particular document. Often these things are not critical to people's lives. Another [Congressional] hearing will do the trick. People generally won't go out of their way to get something.

This librarian expected "the student to learn how to use the library," and was "more interested in imparting that than in getting an answer to every person who wants an answer."

The belief that students should be learning to do their own research is a primary reason why academic librarians do not usually do extensive telephone reference for students, and some public librarians share this attitude. One said that he was "brusque" if a student tried to ask an assignment over the telephone, telling them that "part of the assignment is library research." A public library reference supervisor spoke of a "notable disinclination" to do as much for high school students, and another public librarian said that a question from a child would probably not be considered important enough to forward past the first backup library.

Besides students being able to safely eliminate a particular citation, a topic can be changed to fit the most available information. Stated an academic reference head:

> We don't do as much referral for undergraduate students because they have the leeway in a lot of cases to change topics, and very often you're not changing the topic, but perhaps directing it in a slightly different direction. They're overlimiting what they want to work on, or they haven't figured out a good focus.

A coworker of this person agreed that students' research papers were intended as "more an exercise in research than the content."

Not only is the obtaining of particular material usually not crucial to the success of most written assignments, but also on some campuses written assignments are few. An academic librarian said that "only slowly are we coming back to writing term papers." "Until a few years ago," he noted, "it was common for a student to come here never having written a term paper in high school." At a second academic library it was said that the students did a "lot of laboratory and memorization," with library research playing "only a small role." In a third the lack of referral activity was said to be because "this is an undergraduate school, and most people are taking a fairly 'cut and dried' program." A student at a private college said that he expected to graduate as a business major after having written only one, nine page term paper, for an English course; some shorter English papers; an "opinion" paper; and a seven-page business paper composed mostly of graphs.

Despite the challenges of the shy student, the overdemanding student, the indifferent student, and the student
having few needs other than instruction in library research,
reference librarians do have opportunities to provide maximum in-library assistance and referral. Said the Exemplary
Referrer:

> It depends on how much research oriented the stu-
> dent is. If the student really is anxious to do a
> good job and is willing to travel, those are all fac-
> tors, and the time, and, "Do you have a car?,"
> and, "How much can you spend?," and do they
> really need all this high-powered research or can
> they answer the question with what we have? So
> you have to take all these factors into consideration.

Other academic librarians said that the "persistent" student,
or the one expressing "assertiveness," or a student who is
"really sincerely interested or else desperate for the material,"
would more likely be given extra assistance, including referral advice. Commented a public library reference head:
"With so many of the mentally gaga types that come in from
the schools, to have a bright glow come in, you just over-
load the kid."

Occasionally the librarian serves as a long-term academic mentor, leading to carefully chosen referrals. The
following quotation describes such a situation:

> Sometimes you develop relationships with students.
> The student actually is living here four years, and
> you begin to--it's not uncommon the student comes
> back on a regular basis. They tend to be the more
> sophisticated student, so by the time they're maybe
> senior or even junior, they tend to do a very much
> more elaborate kind of study. This is unusual but
> it happens. You know that the student is already
> pursuing a level of work, so that you want to en-
> courage them to use the major collections--the
> [major library]. You want to expose them to the
> fact that as big as they thought this place was,
> there is even a better one.

This librarian also said to broaden the horizons of the
less academically sophisticated: "I like to give students too

much information because if the student's general presumption about the library because of their inadequate skill at finding material is that there is never enough, and if you convince them that there's more than enough, then you've done an important job in showing them that it's here if they'd only pursue it." He could tell when students felt overwhelmed by his suggestions: "You watch their eyes. They get glassy."

Not all librarians agreed with the earlier mentioned comment that it is more important to have the student learn to use the library than to obtain a specific answer. One stated, "We do that in our library instruction program, but if someone comes to us with a reference question, we try to help them find the answer to the reference question." Even the librarian who made the earlier statement said that he was careful not to refer students to another documents depository without "pinpointing the document" first so that they do not "spend half the day playing around" with an index when they reach the library referred to. Perhaps the least feeling that the student is responsible for his own research was evidenced by a librarian who said online bibliographic searching was being promoted for the following reason: "Our students are not going to be going out into the world and be hitting the books. They should be asking their special librarian to do a computer search for them." To sum up, librarians have different attitudes towards students, but in general they have had at least some experience with interested students whom they have advised with referrals.

Academic librarians also deal with faculty, an interaction having its own set of problems. One librarian complained that "there is a sort of unwritten policy where faculty is treated like royalty." An academic library supervisor claimed that no distinction in service was made "between freshman and faculty," and this ideal may be as common in academic libraries as the corresponding one in public libraries that every request is treated equally, but in practice requests from faculty often do take priority.

Turning the focus to public libraries, a diverse range of users is apparent. A number of discrete clienteles are served, and these clienteles can change as the community's social and economic composition changes. At an urban library

in an area experiencing an influx of wealthier residents, a
librarian noted:

> There is a tide, and they wash out of the houses
> in the morning. Sometimes when I arrive at nine
> o'clock you'll see the tail end, attache cases and
> three-piece suits. Very nice.

These newcomers made heavy use of the library's local history collection. At the same library an influx of immigrants
necessitated use of a backup library which had books in
their language, and referrals to government agencies.
Elsewhere a librarian who had worked in a branch library
in an impoverished area also made many referrals to agencies. In a middle class community, a public librarian said
that the elderly often sought the address of companies con-
nected to their financial investments.

As in academic libraries, not all users of public libraries are dedicated to pursuing information. One public
librarian commented:

> If anything limited referrals, I'd say it's the patron
> himself because they don't want to go too far,
> physically; they don't want to travel too far. They
> don't want it to take too long, and they don't want
> it to cost anything.... They want it now, and they
> want it right there [snap fingers] and then, or they
> want to be able to walk down the block and get it.

A user's unwillingness to travel or a lack of direct
borrowing privileges at other libraries may make interlibrary loan seem like a logical alternative to referral. However, interlibrary loan is frequently too slow, especially
for students, and in some libraries comments were made that
promoting it would be the ideal, but that processing more
loan requests would require too much of the staff's time.
In a couple of small public libraries, on the other hand,
interlibrary loan was said to be offered and used often.
In a large public library a reference head, suggesting that
the lack of promotion of interlibrary loan is caused more by
librarians' poor attitudes than by legitimate time considerations, stated, "We plug people into a service company without ever telling them that's what they're for, you know, to
be extending of themselves, and to offer service, and they

get into an attitude resembling somebody at a social service
agency: 'Well, these people are entitled to this, but I'll
be dammed if I'm going to tell them they're entitled to this
too.'"

    While librarians in smaller libraries seemed more likely
to be heavily involved in interlibrary loan, demand for referral is slight in small branches of public libraries, according to interviewees with experience in them, because users
generally bypassed them if the request was of the type that
would require referral. In contrast, at a large public library the following statement was made:

> I should say that patrons come to the desk and say,
> "If you don't have this information, can you refer
> me to either an individual or an institution that has
> it." I think that many of our patrons do recognize
> the limitations of this particular institution, and
> freely expect that we'll serve as a clearinghouse
> for information if you will tell them where to go.

    As in academic libraries, the overly demanding or ob-
noxious user must be faced. Librarians differed as to
whether such people should receive more or less assistance.
One public librarian said she would "tend to turn off to
arrogant and demanding people, and to be less helpful, I'm
sure, and the kids who say, 'Miss!,' don't get much help
from me." She also suggested that she would do "less and
more" for such people: "To get them out of my hair, I'll
send them some place else." Another librarian also stated,
"If they're really obnoxious we might say, 'Well, call such
and such a place,' instead of us doing it."

    Elsewhere, however, a librarian contended that "the
squeaky wheel, the demanding patron, gets attention," while
in another location a librarian said that if a person were ob-
noxiously overdemanding she would "bend over backwards to
not let that get in the way." One librarian warned that "the
worse the patron is, the worse they're going to be if you
fluff them off, so you have to give them some kind of answer, and present it in such a way that you are very definite." He described how he would go through the steps of
looking for information in his library even if he thought from
the beginning that it would not be found and that a referral
would be necessary because he felt: "If you immediately

say, 'Go here,' or 'Go there,' they don't believe you.
They think you're trying to get rid of them."

Despite protestations that everyone receives equal
service, librarians at times provide service based on the
importance of the requester. Mention was made of an extra
effort being extended for city officials. One librarian
stated that work for city officials was done even though
the subject would ordinarily be transferred to a different
department of the library because a supervisor "thought we
would do a good job of it." Admitting that more would be
done for a middle-aged businessman, one public librarian
confessed:

> I feel guilty saying things like that. We're not
> supposed to make any distinctions about who the
> user is, but in practice there's no way we can get
> all of our work done without [drawing] some lines
> some place.

Another type of status is accorded physical attractiveness. Both academic and public librarians were questioned
briefly about this, except for a few instances in which it
was felt enough sensitive topics had been discussed and
broaching another one might create a less responsive atmosphere.

One librarian admitted that he and a coworker had
once discussed the issue, concluding first that "if somebody
is nice and pleasant, congenial, you'll be more prone to
help them than if somebody is kind of cranky and demanding"; and second that if "somebody is physically more at-
tractive" it is "just human nature" for librarians to "go out
of their way to help than if somebody comes in; they're
really creepy looking and kinda--; then you want to get rid
of them." Addressing an equity issue, he concluded: "It
may not be fair, but we came to the earth-shattering conclusion that it was just human nature, that probably most
people would do that."

Several other librarians also felt that physical attractiveness could be a factor, but in general they linked it to
a user having a pleasant personality too. The only interviewee who did not state that personality would have to be
a contributing factor claimed that physical attractiveness is

"not critical in terms of reference service." Most of those
admitting that physical attractiveness was a factor made
some allusion to equity considerations, such as that they
were admitting a "prejudice" or that it would not be "professional" if they allowed themselves to be too influenced.
However, only one librarian made an unequivocal response
that the "dress or look" of a user "does not affect my reference work."

In summary, the conversations held in this study indicated that most librarians accept at least in part the ethical prescription that users should be treated equally, but
the actual practice of the principle is complicated by num-
erous factors. One is the social norm that people should
work for what they get. How much, then, is owed to the
student who acts lazy or indifferent? Some understanding
and skillful librarians will work past their own annoyance
and try to awaken the disinterested and draw out the shy.
Even when helping an articulate, motivated student, the
librarian must decide if the omission of a fact or a citation,
or a change in topic, is the wiser course as long as the
student is learning how to do research, or whether the student should be challenged by referral to specialized collections seeking specific answers to the original question.

Librarians are faced with deciding what it means to be
human, and what it means to be a professional. How much
abuse should be taken from an obnoxious user before less
service is provided? How much extra effort should be allowed when the user's personality or appearance are appeal-
ing?

Practical considerations can weigh heavily on the librarian's conscience, especially if he or she is very busy.
Is a student's request really equal to that of a business-
person's? Considering the benefits to the library of pleasing
city officials, should their requests be accorded special
handling?

Attitudes About Distance and
About Travel Information

The issue of distance was seen as having a large effect on referral. One of the most generalizable findings of
this study, which was conducted in areas of relatively high

population density, is that librarians select from possible places to refer with convenience of travel in mind.

In some cases librarians offered choices to users. A public librarian stated, "I usually give them the options because some people don't know anything about [town], and they're more directed toward [other town], so I try to give them the options of what they're most familiar with or what might be more convenient for them." Here knowledge of geography and of libraries listed is helpful for quickly locating which library is most convenient. However, librarians also simply may ask the user to name convenient locations.

Students' access to automobiles is a consideration. Reference librarians in two academic libraries situated near a city said that students without cars naturally preferred referral to the city's libraries. In a more suburban environment, an academic librarian said that "there seem to be students with cars who can get other students to where they need to go." In a suburban public library, it was said that "most everybody" has a car.

Librarians can hardly help but be conscious of the convenience factor since users do not hide their unwillingness to spend time traveling. One academic librarian said that some undergraduates would sooner switch topics than be referred to another library half an hour away by public transportation. On the other hand, graduate students were said to be willing to "go anywhere." One librarian stated that a local periodicals union list was used first for undergraduates, who generally don't have automobiles, while the state list was used with graduate students.

It seems that at times librarians may be making decisions based on misperceptions of the general willingness of people to travel. Librarians in neighboring public libraries gave opposite opinions regarding users' willingness to travel to New York City. Said a librarian in the smaller of the two libraries: "I suggested New York Public Library to one or two people. Neither time was it well received. No one wanted to make the trip to New York." A librarian in a neighboring backup library, however, said regarding whether people will go to the City: "They do. Someone's father may work in New York, or the wife will go in with him one

day to use Lincoln Center. we've made a referral there."
In another library, very close to Manhattan, people's willingness to go there was taken for granted. Said one librarian:

> People say to us, "I'll go to Forty-Second Street
> [New York Public Library] if you don't have
> it...." So we refer to [backup library], and our
> patrons refer themselves to New York if they feel
> like it.

At variance with librarians' attempts to refer users
to convenient locations was an apparent widespread inability
or unwillingness to provide adequate travel directions to
those locations. More often than not interviewees responded
vaguely on this matter. One head of reference said "maybe" when asked if there was a bus schedule to one of the
libraries she referred to most often. In another library an
interviewee said he was not sure if there was a bus to the
library to which most referrals were made, and in a third
library a bus schedule was said to be kept at the reference
desk but could not be found.

Asked if she could give directions to the only nearby
major medical library in her state, a reference supervisor
said she could not, adding: "It hasn't happened that often,
and then we can give the address. Well, maybe somebody
downstairs would be able to give directions." Another librarian in the same library said she could not give a precise
description of how to reach the backup research library,
noting that "at one time" there had been maps made up.
An interviewee in another library was also unable to give
directions to the medical library, saying that he was only
asked for them "once in a while" since most users had lived
in the area all their lives. Opinion on ease of public transportation to a large city differed in one library, with a
reference librarian thinking it was simple and the director
thinking it was quite complicated. Elsewhere a librarian on
the job over half a year had not visited the public library,
perhaps a fifteen minute walk away, "thinks" it's within
walking distance, and "thinks" she knows the street it is on.

There was a lesser amount of encouraging responses
on this subject. One administrator said that her head of
reference, influenced by previous experience in a special

library, would emphasize the principle of knowing where the other library is (along with knowing what they have, having comfortable relations with them, and using the telephone if that is best). The previously mentioned Exemplary Referrer was able to give quick, precise information about street names, train connections, number of train stops to a destination, and number of blocks between stop and destination. One reference head was able to say what route a bus took and within how many blocks it passed from several libraries. Another head of reference said he photocopies a street map as needed when giving directions. For a different perspective, it was learned from a supervisor of an Alcoholics Anonymous hotline that he was able to give driving directions to the over 150 AA meeting locations in his region.

To summarize, librarians are usually efficient enough to send a user to a closer resource rather than to a more distant one. Some of the disagreement regarding users' willingness to travel suggests that this willingness could be interpreted either way, depending on whether and how the librarian suggests the outside resource. Similarly, graduate students' apparent greater willingness to travel may be due not only to higher motivation, narrower disciplinary focus, or higher program expectations, but also to librarians' expectations that they should be willing to travel.

Perhaps the most obvious failing in talking to librarians was their inability to give directions to the places to which they referred. While this task can be complicated by consideration of travel from a direction other than from the referring library, some basic information is not too difficult to write down and keep handy. Copies of maps showing routes to other libraries also seem advantageous, although they might bring fears of an inequitable overpromotion of use of these libraries.

By suggesting the closest available location when they refer, librarians give evidence of concern for efficient use of the user's time. Just why this concern does not extend more often to giving travel directions is difficult to say. Perhaps referral is so infrequent that librarians do not bother with learning or keeping aids to provide directions. It seems more likely that librarians simply see such an effort as beyond the responsibility of their library, more than the user is owed. Even with such an equity orientation, it is

puzzling that librarians do not relate the frustration they
must have felt at times in getting lost when trying to reach
an unfamiliar destination to problems the user must experience.

Attitudes About Travel Safety

Fear as a factor influencing referral was an unex-
pected finding, but in retrospect it is not an illogical result
since major libraries, especially larger and older public ones,
are often in cities having reputations for street crime. Users may feel that the cost in terms of personal risk is not
worth the danger of visiting such locations. The librarian
faces a delicate equity decision: Does fairness to the user
require some words of caution even at the risk of appearing
unduly alarmist or further contributing to the isolation of
central cities?

At one suburban academic library, interviewees stated
that users "laugh at the idea of going" to a nearby city
library, and are "all suburbanites" who expect "to be mur-
dered in the street." At a public library in a wealthy community, a librarian said she did not refer "too much" to a
nearby backup library since "people get hysterical because
they don't want to go" there. At another public library it
was said that the effect of a cooperative borrowing system
was that users were switching to libraries considered to be
in safer communities. In one urban public library a librarian
said that users from poor neighborhoods expressed no fear
in coming to the library, but that people living in a middle
class section of the city find the neighborhood surrounding
the library "very upsetting."

Sometimes urban librarians feel that travel to downtown areas is risky, but do not feel threatened near their
own location. Staff at one city's main library believed that
a branch library in a busier and more accessible section enjoyed an undeserved reputation for being safer. One librarian conceded that the main library, unlike the branch,
had "groups of people: unemployed, drunken, or sometimes on drugs" on nearby sidewalks, but she did not "find
that they generally bother people."

It is not easy to tell how much of users' fears may
actually be induced by librarians. At the only library

where librarians said users were not afraid to travel to
inner cities, they were said to be mostly male and used to
an urban environment. Also, not many referrals were
made to areas considered dangerous. One of the librarians,
however, confessed that she would be "very nervous" walking in one city, and "may project a certain nervousness"
when suggesting others go there. In another location a
female librarian stated that in recent years she had not
noticed students being fearful about travel to a downtown
library, while a male librarian found "considerable hesitation
on the part of a lot of these students, especially females."
The female librarian thought, incorrectly, that the downtown
library no longer had evening hours so that her referrals
were only for the safer daytime hours. It is possible, however, that the male librarian was more solicitous about the
female students than was his female coworker, who had
worked in an inner-city library and felt that if she could
"cope" with such situations, "other people should be able
to too."

Similarly, in a library located in an area which the
staff admitted "was not the safest" and one librarian was
"petrified" to take public transportation at night, the head
of reference said that suburbanites would "do anything" to
avoid traveling to a larger public library nearby; yet in
the same library was a librarian who was a member of a
minority group and who said that no one had expressed
reluctance to her about going to the larger library. It
seems possible that some users were instinctively fearful or
some were concerned that the minority-group librarian might
think comments about crime were racially motivated, but also
that the reference head has fostered some of the fear.

Granted that most of the librarians interviewed perceive some danger, the question is what to do about it in
the referral process. Should users be warned? About twice
as many librarians said that they would offer some warnings
as said they would not. The issue is approached with care
by some. One librarian advised the interviewer that walking
to a nearby library while wearing a suit and carrying a
briefcase was dangerous, noting that a bus could be taken
instead. Asked if he would give the same warning to the
public, he stated, "We're supposed to pretend that it's not
an issue." He said that if a caller asking for directions to
his library sounded like a young woman he might suggest
coming by car rather than by bus. However, he continued:

> Unless I know the person I'm talking to, you can't
> tell people that. They take it the wrong way.
> They think you're saying something negative about
> the people who live here.

Several librarians said that they cautioned people
planning to go to an urban library at night. Young women
and old people were more likely to be warned, and the trip
would not be advised for a "young kid." Advice might be
given regarding parking. A public librarian admitted:

> Maybe I do volunteer too much sometimes. For in-
> stance if it's a middle-aged or older woman who
> wants to copy something from the New York Times,
> I would say, "Why don't you try [nearby academic
> library] first before you try [urban] library," be-
> cause I know it's safer up there.

In terms of equity, librarians who give warnings apparently feel that the user is owed protection, even at the
cost of appearing prejudiced or alarmist. In addition, the
last quotation points to the further equity issue of the burden of providing service being shifted from urban libraries
that receive financial aid for serving as backup libraries to
libraries that are not so funded, or the possible inequitous
impact on the reputation of the library in the urban setting.

Librarians who said that they would not provide warnings pose equity issues also. For one thing, offering alternatives to users can have the same effect as explicit warnings. One librarian said that "a lot of people" did not like
going to an inner-city backup library, and if she suggested
it at the same time that she suggested a private, suburban
academic library, "people are much more willing" to go to the
latter. Yet when asked if she would warn people about going to the city library at night, she said: "Oh no, no.
I would be talking to people who know the city better than
I do."

A young public librarian, asked if he cautioned users
about going to an inner-city backup library, recoiled:

> No, No. God! I won't say that. I'd get in trou-
> ble. No, no. I wouldn't do that. I just tell them.
> I tell them where it is, you know. They say,

"Where is it?" I say [street with bad reputation],
and then if they're from the area, they know where
it is.

Asked if he would not warn a woman about traveling there
at night, he replied, "If they've just moved into the area,
or for whatever reasons they don't know the [city] area,
it's easier just to tell them to try a closer library." Here,
again, there is an instance of shifting the service burden
away from the designated backup library. As for this librarian's fear of being reprimanded, he might have been
overreacting because other librarians in the same library
did caution users about traveling at night. If he was not
overreacting, his coworkers appear to have chosen to as-
sert their independence, feeling that they had the right to
provide warnings in consideration of the protection owed the
user.

There were several sites where it appeared that a lack
of travel information, bus schedules, maps, and so on for
directing users to urban backup libraries was a silent means
of reducing the likelihood of what was considered to be an
unsafe trip. When asked if frankness regarding safety and
provision of advice on safest times and routes would not be
the best approach, the director of an urban academic library
said that it would be a problem because of the sensitive nature of the topic. This is unfortunate because becoming lost
in a strange city is often a greater danger than taking a
well traveled route to a center-city library. A response to
the safety issue that would seem to indicate a librarian's
overconcern with her own welfare was that of a librarian
who said she personally felt safe taking the train to a nearby city, but if a user expressed fear of going there she
would not offer an opinion regarding the safest times to
travel because she did not "want them to come back and say
they got mugged."

Sometimes not discussing the safety issue is a way of
denigrating the user's fear. An older librarian in a public
library considered to be in a somewhat unsafe area said that
some people would say that they did not want to go to a
neighboring city. Asked how she replied to such statements, she responded in a soothing voice: "It's not hard to
get to. It's right on [street]. Easy to get to." Told that
people were probably not worried about being able to find

the library, she replied, "Not really," and laughed heartily,
adding: "People don't want to come to [her library], if
you want to know. That's true. Oh, that's true."

   In summary it was found that fear is an issue in referral. Some of the librarians appear, consciously or un-
consciously, to discourage referral travel to cities with large
poor minority populations. Some inner-city librarians believe that since they cope with urban problems, potential
users can too. They feel that exaggerations about dangers
are inequitable to themselves and to their libraries.

   Perhaps most inequitable is any absence of printed
travel directions showing routes and parking. Such aids
could perhaps help insure the user's safety and increase
the use of urban libraries, but seem not to be provided in
part because librarians find it more comfortable to ignore a
sensitive subject. About two-thirds of librarians interviewed
did say that they would give some warning or advice regarding safety.

   Another type of inequity is the additional workload
shifted to libraries in middle-class suburbs when people are
afraid to visit the urban libraries, the latter frequently being those which receive state funding to serve as backup
facilities. Librarians who do not discuss the fear factor
directly with users still contribute to this shift when they
suggest the suburban libraries in lieu of or as alternatives
to the urban ones.

Feedback from Users

   By receiving feedback, a librarian may learn if an
answer or referral was useful, which can be an aid in improving future referral. This topic will be divided into discussions of librarians receiving no feedback, little feedback,
or much feedback; and also the subject of organized feedback.

   No feedback. In general, librarians interviewed received little or no feedback. An assertion of no feedback
was made by at least one librarian in each of the ten participating libraries, except for the two smallest of the five
public libraries. Said one individual, "The crazy thing
about referral is the feedback because you almost never

know what happened." Even asking for feedback did not
work for another person. Regarding a museum service for
identifying objects, he said, "I used to ask them, 'Please
call me to let me know what happened,' and never, never--
no one ever called back." One academic librarian reported:
"You really have to grab the kid if you see him again and
say, 'Did you get the answer from the place? Did you
call?'" Another academic librarian said that the "nice thing
about faculty work" was the feedback, in contrast to working with undergraduates.

Lack of feedback may be interpreted as an indication
that there are no problems. One librarian wondered whether
"the feedback is we don't have complaints, so would that be
a good indication that what we're doing has to be either
right or--?" Similarly, another librarian when asked if he
had received feedback responded: "I can't say that I have.
They come back and use your brain again, which may mean
you did a good job the first time"; and a third librarian
also said feedback existed in the sense that "somebody else
I've helped will refer a person to me."

Little feedback. Some librarians received occasional
feedback, as was the case with everyone interviewed at the
next to smallest public library, serving basically a local
clientele. The director said feedback was more likely to
come from a person "who uses the library a lot and is used
to making comments." The head of reference made the unusual assertion that if an answer is not found, some determined users call back to say where they found the information. One of her subordinates said that once in a while
feedback occurs if a user comes back for something else
and happens to see her, or she sees them and asks, "How
did that go?" Less feedback took place in the more impersonal atmosphere of a large public library, where a librarian
stated:

> If the patron on the phone is friendly, I will ask
> them to call back to say what happened. In ten
> years, one to three called back, saying they had
> contacted the agency and were pleased.

One of the more useful instances of feedback that was
cited may have been that of teachers returning from visits
to a state agency with the information that it would loan

them microfiche readers. Some of the occasional negative
feedback, such as students saying that they "weren't too
welcome" at a very small public library, can assist the librarian in future referrals. At times the feedback is negative but the referral itself cannot be faulted, as when a
student went to another library to use a periodical and
found the needed pages torn out. A librarian saw no reme-
dy: "Even if you check holdings, you don't check for the
pages of an article. You check for the book on the shelf."

   Much feedback. It was noted that at the next to
smallest public library, all librarians received some feedback.
It seems likely that the familiar and more cozy atmosphere
of the smaller setting leads to more conversation with users
and hence more feedback. This suggestion is reinforced by
the fact that at the smallest library, also a public library,
all three reference librarians reported much feedback, versus a finding of no more than one librarian receiving much
feedback in any of the other libraries. One of the three
agreed that library size was a factor, noting, "I think you
seldom see the same person when you're in a large library
with a large staff, and people at the desk are changing so
often that you don't see the same person when you come
in."

   But another factor besides size was apparent. Stated
the second of the three:

        Some people are very grateful, or if they call up
        and ask for a book that we don't have, they'll say,
        "Oh, several months ago you were very helpful and
        got such and such a book for me from a library in
        Florida, and I'd like you to try to get this one for
        me." They let you know that they appreciate it.

The third said:

        Our patrons think the sun rises and sets on us, for
        the most part. We have people who will come up
        and they'll talk to us and sit.... We rarely get
        bad feedback. They really do like what we do,
        and we really do try to go as far as they want us
        to go for the material.

The additional factor is service. Interlibrary loan especially

was promoted much more heavily than in the other libraries,
resulting in expressions of gratitude from users.

Five other librarians reported considerable feedback,
but size of library or extent of service did not seem to be
the major factor. These five impressed this interviewer as
having a pleasant and in some cases empathic manner likely
to put a user at ease. Three of the five said that they
receive compliments, with one commenting:

> Usually people say, "You've been so helpful to me
> before, I hope you can help me again," or when
> they leave they say: "Thank you so much for your
> help. You've been heaven sent; God bless you."

A fourth said that people often said that they found exact-
ly what they wanted, but "sometimes they complain." A
fifth said that rather than dealing with undergraduates,
who "tend to be rather timid," she dealt mainly with graduate students: "They tell me, 'I didn't get this here. Now
what?' So we renegotiate, or they say they did find it--
'Thank you!'"

It may be significant that all five of these librarians
were women. Of the librarians who were tape recorded in
one of the ten participating libraries, only 1 of the 12 men
but 4 of the 22 women were in the much feedback category,
versus 6 (50%) of the men and 6 (27%) of the women in the
no feedback category. It may be that women are more likely
to project or be perceived as possessing greater empathy
and thus interest in the user, a possibility that will be returned to in a literature review in the next chapter.

Organized feedback. Since most librarians experienced
little or no feedback, and since it seems likely that feedback
can improve service, it might be expected that there would
be support for an organized system of supplying feedback.
A few examples of existing rule-governed feedback were
encountered. One librarian, who received such feedback
regarding her interlibrary loan requests but not her referrals said, "The only time I've been called to correct something
is when I've done something incorrectly on my ILL form, not
for sending someone some place." Another librarian had
been corrected regarding her interlibrary loan forms, and
also for sending a question to a backup library "phrased in

a way that they don't approve of, or whatever." He felt
that he should be corrected, stating, "I don't want to keep
doing it wrong." A third librarian felt that one research
library was too exacting in its criticisms of the way she
filled out network access passes.

A system of issuing permission slips to borrow from a
research library was said to result in "quite a bit" of feedback when students returned, with most of them saying that
they found what they needed, but a few claiming that the
material was not what they expected, or that material that
was supposed to be there could not be located. An unusual
form of feedback from students was cited by a librarian who
taught classes in research skills at a college. He received
a copy of each student's "final presentation, to see what
they have finally worked on, and that's interesting because
it's a real follow-through."

While most of the above librarians seemed to approve
of existing feedback mechanisms relating to their own performance, about an equal number of those interviewed had
doubts about organized feedback. One librarian said that a
system of passes for entry to other libraries, allowing the
referrer to be identified and corrected in cases of erroneous
referral, "just strikes me as more red tape to go through,
more little forms to fill out, more statistics to collect."
Another librarian stated:

> It depends on how it's used. I can see that it
> would be very annoying to work in a large library
> that gets a lot of referrals mistakenly.... I'd just
> hate to think that it would be used--"Mr. Jones
> did this, this, and this," and have it more a per-
> sonal attack on the person. If done just in the
> interest of accuracy, I don't think it's so bad. It's
> like the verification requirement in interloan. We
> return things to people who don't submit complete
> information.

A small public library's director, who had a poor
opinion of his backup library, thought that it would be
"upset" if it were evaluated, as by a system of users returning postcards on which they had written evaluations.
Another librarian believed that "those people who are very
suspicious and resentful would look at a form where someone

is going to check you in the most negative light possible,
I'm sure, but someone else who is relatively unconcerned
about these kinds of things" would "take it in stride."
One very suspicious person was encountered. She refused
to be interviewed and denounced the research as "spying."

To summarize, feedback in the sense of a report coming back about how a user fared at an outside resource
referred to seems to be rare. Thus feedback cannot be
very significant in improving referral. The prospect of
organized feedback to improve referrals makes some librarians uncomfortable, but similar approaches in the handling
of interlibrary loan and cooperative reference suggest that
there need not be much cause for worry. In equity terms
librarians may be exhibiting too much concern for themselves and not enough for what is due their users.

Feedback in the sense of compliments for services
completed within the library, rather than for referral, is
more frequent. It seems more likely to occur when extra
service is extended, as in heavily promoted interlibrary
loan. A smaller library with only a few librarians rotating
at the reference desk also appears to be conducive to an
atmosphere of friendly conversation and positive feedback.

In addition, a greater degree of feedback was reported by several female librarians whose personalities this
researcher felt conveyed pleasantness and empathy. From
an equity standpoint, it could be said that kind compliments are felt to be owed to those who exude kindness,
but from another perspective it could be stated that such
people are approached for pleasant small talk because they
are receptive and easy to talk to. Most positive feedback
may not teach the librarian anything new, but it probably
serves as a morale booster.

Summary of Factors Concerning the User

Librarians vary in their skill in determining users'
needs and in their patience in dealing with difficult users'
attitudes. Equity judgments regarding users' deservedness
were described. Distance to outside resources is a key
consideration for both librarians and their clientele, but
librarians seemed insufficiently prepared to provide adequate
travel directions. A particular service offered is advice

regarding urban dangers, which has equity implications for
struggling city libraries that lose potential patrons and for
suburban libraries to which these users turn.

Feedback from users, a potentially important source
of information about services provided by outside resources
and about the accuracy of referrals, was not a common experience for most of those interviewed. When it occurred
it consisted mainly of gratitude for the complete servicing
of a request rather than for a referral. The infrequency
of organized feedback pertaining to referrals was ascribed
in part to some librarians' concern over having their errors
exposed.

PRIMARY RELATIONSHIPS AND VARIABLES

The many factors that have been described in this
chapter as relating to library referral are listed in the
Table of Contents of this study. They are six personal
qualities: efficiency, equity, achievement motivation, empathy, tact, and independence; factors concerning the potential referrer's library: interaction with the director,
interaction with coworkers, extent of training and experience, activity level at the reference desk, collection
strength, and availability and use of referral tools; factors
concerning outside resources: strength and knowledge of
outside resources, impersonal relations with outside resources, extent of personal contacts, and interaction with
faculty (in academic libraries); and factors concerning the
user: evaluation of the user, attitudes about distance and
about travel information, attitudes about travel safety, and
feedback from the user.

Suggesting a relationship among the separate factors
is simplified once it is recognized that they all can relate to
effective referral. It readily can be seen that those factors
that are oriented towards the librarian's own library could
be associated with effectiveness. Thus, a director who pro-
motes referral, a training program, other educational experiences, supportive coworkers, enough staff at the reference
desk, an awareness of weaknesses in the collection, and
good indexes and directories all might contribute to meeting
the user's need.

Similarly, the factors associated with outside resources may contribute to effective referral. Strong external resources and knowledge of their strengths, receptive
personnel and policies at other institutions, personal contacts, and a close working relationship with faculty seem
likely to promote effective referral. Finally, the factors
oriented towards the user may contribute when the librarian
evaluates the user's needs accurately, provides directions
to convenient facilities to meet needs, gives helpful advice
regarding safe ways to travel, and receives accurate feedback.

Efficiency in the sense of saving the user time or
money enhances effective referral, but librarians must also
consider the cost of referral, primarily in time, to themselves. This consideration was evident in the areas of
training, providing sufficient staff at the reference desk,
creating referral files and travel instructions, cultivating
outside contacts, interacting with faculty, giving careful
service to users and seeking feedback. it was evident also
in the referral-related activities of interlibrary loan and of
telephoning to obtain materials or answers to reference
questions. All these activities take time and must be
weighed against other important library functions. Furthermore, what is efficient for the user may be inefficient for
an outside resource upon which a demand is being placed.

Efficiency, then, frequently relates to the concept
of equity. Librarians must decide, given available time
and resources, what users, both individually and collective-
ly, deserve in terms of referral services.

Achievement motivation is presumed to underlie much
of the librarian's efforts to make an effective and efficient
referral. It may also be linked to the librarian's feeling of
independence in that sometimes rules are ignored to achieve
an objective. Librarians who told of ignoring their director's orders or ignoring network protocols gave evidence of
an independence that raises equity issues.

Empathy for the user appeared to be related to
achievement motivation in that it can mitigate the boredom
of repetitive tasks that otherwise might provide little satisfaction. It also might be related to equity because the
strict accounting that may be felt to be required by equity

can appear callous to one who is empathetic. Some may feel
that the service orientation of librarianship requires a degree of empathy towards the user. If empathy is not required, the minimum requirement seemed to be tact, which
the librarian may be said to both owe and be owed in equitable relationships with fellow employees, users and outsiders. Lack of tact presumably can make an easy task difficult and is therefore inefficient.

The librarian, therefore, is likely to be aided in referral by having certain personal qualities. Qualities of
achievement motivation, efficiency, and tact, and possibly
independence and empathy, appear to be required for a
high level of achievement. Studying these as virtues to be
acquired, however, is not sufficient. Hard choices must be
made regarding equity.

EQUITY AS THE CORE VARIABLE

It is the notion that equity is the primary conceptual
basis of referral that is the principal finding. It is, in
this study, the "core" variable said in the section on "General Methodological Principles" above (p. 13) to have been
espoused by Glaser (1978) for giving coherence to research
results. As stated above (p. 28), equity here has the
meaning of a just and fair distribution of valued resources,
with "resources" meaning any valued condition.

It is strongly evident in the factors oriented towards
the user. The very notion of evaluating the user in terms
of deservedness would strike some as offending equity.
Part of the evaluation is concerned with the tactful treatment the user is thought to owe to the librarian.

The consideration of distance relates to equity in the
sense that the most geographically convenient library may
not be the one funded to serve outsiders. Offering the
user adequate travel instructions to reach a place referred
to apparently is not something many librarians feel an obligation to provide, although they may also fear being viewed
as freeloaders if they go so far as to have printed travel
instructions ready to hand out. In addition, advising about
safety has strong equity implications for the user, who is
owed the right to survive; for the institution warned about;

and for institutions in safer areas receiving an influx of users who are afraid to visit urban locations.

Feedback, in an organized sense, is generally absent in part because librarians felt that they are owed protection from its possibly embarrassing results. Spontaneous feedback is uncommon, perhaps because users feel they do not owe it to librarians except to thank one who has provided extraordinary service or who has been especially pleasant.

Equity is a strong component of most of the factors related to outside resources. In deciding on the desirability of these resources, the librarian's simple and generally true equation of large libraries with needed materials puts a heavy burden on these libraries. Lack of knowledge of outside resources, seen in the area of documents collections, means that users may not get the service due them.

The friendliness or receptivity of outside resources is generally viewed as largely conditioned by the reasonableness of the demands made upon them. Overloading the receptive library with needless requests can end its friendliness. Apparent generosity, it seems, is usually based on the expectation of favors done in return, either directly by the institution being served, or by some other institution acting as a sort of proxy for the one actually incurring the debt. Personal contacts were found to owe each other extra effort. In academic institutions, faculty who unnecessarily refer to outside libraries are seen as shortchanging on-campus libraries and overburdening the other institutions.

As for factors relating to one's own library, the director's concern for what is owed the user or for what is owed the library in terms of good public relations may conflict with the librarians' feelings regarding a right to make personal judgments on how to provide service without overloading themselves or outside resources.

The equity aspect of training in connection with the user being owed a service by librarians well trained in referral seems but weakly formulated in most libraries. This is despite the fact that librarians consider a training process that includes tactful correcting of their errors to be desirable. Nonprofessionals expected to provide some reference service seem to be more likely to be slighted in terms of referral instruction. They are also sometimes scorned by librarians for attempting reference or referral work for which they are not trained, an attempt that may awake not only librarians' concern for the user's interest but also for their own status as trained professionals with the right to perform certain functions.

Coworkers are consulted by librarians out of equity for all concerned: due respect is tendered the coworker, the user is provided the most convenient service, and other institutions are not unnecessarily overtaxed. Most librarians seemed willing to admit ignorance in the interest of the service owed to the user, but at least one librarian's sense of tact prevented him from exposing a coworker's error in order to meet a user's need. Some coworkers are described as not being interested in general reference work, feeling that it is an intrusion on their rightful duties.

Being too busy at the reference desk may cause referrals, creating an unfair demand on outside resources. It may also leave the librarian with the feeling of being unfairly overworked and the user being unfairly neglected. A weak collection can be viewed as an indication that the user is being deprived and neighboring libraries with better collections are being relied upon to an inequitable extent. In addition, some librarians are embarrassed by working with a poor collection, while others made the argument that funding is inequitable, and still others have relatively little difficulty in accepting the need to refer, especially if there is a funded backup library nearby. Regarding indexes and directories, some librarians may be too hesitant to share their individual reference and referral card files.

Equity, then, is the major variable, interweaving with and confusing as it does the other major consideration, efficiency. Equity asks what users, outside resources, personal contacts, coworkers, the director, and the individual librarian owe and are owed. Efficiency accentuates equity by asking what limitations must be imposed on what is owed due to the scarcity of resources. What have scholars said about equity and its alternatives? This is the question to be answered in the next chapter.

CHAPTER 4

THE LITERATURE REGARDING EQUITY

INTRODUCTION

Following the discovery that the interview data pointed to equity as a key consideration in librarians' referrals, the literature concerning equity was examined to see how it relates to the results presented in the previous chapter. Examined first is equity as viewed by most social psychologists, followed by two alternative views: that of Lawrence Kohlberg, and that of two authors who describe an attitude of caring.

EQUITY AND THE SOCIAL PSYCHOLOGISTS

In the literature of social psychology, the meaning given equity is usually that of a balance between what one contributes and what one receives. A cynical perspective is presented by Walster, Walster, and Berschied (1978), who believe that, given the opportunity, people would accept benefits and avoid making contributions.

They begin with the following propositions:

PROPOSITION I: Individuals will try to maximize their outcomes (where outcomes equal rewards minus costs).

111

> PROPOSITION IIA: Groups can maximize collec-
> tive reward by evolving accepted systems for equit-
> ably apportioning resources among members. Thus,
> groups will evolve such systems of equity, and will
> attempt to induce members to accept and adhere to
> these systems.
> PROPOSITION IIB: Groups will generally reward
> members who treat others equitably, and generally
> punish (increase the cost for) members who treat
> others inequitably.
> PROPOSITION III: When individuals find them-
> selves participating in inequitable relationships,
> they will become distressed. The more inequitable
> the relationship, the more distress individuals will
> feel.
> PROPOSITION IV: Individuals who discover they
> are in an inequitable relationship will attempt to
> eliminate their distress by restoring equity. The
> greater the inequity that exists, the more distress
> they will feel, and the harder they will try to re-
> store equity. (p. 6)

Walster et al. write that their theory "rests on the
simple, but eminently safe, assumption that man is selfish"
(p. 7). They quote Blau (1968, p. 453): "To be sure,
there are men who unselfishly work for others without
thought of reward and even without expecting gratitude,
but these are virtually saints, and saints are rare" (p.
101). Walster et al. wish to correct those who assume that
"the laboriously learned principle that one must behave
equitably, or suffer, somehow gains a life of its own," so
that if "it becomes a more profitable strategy to be totally
selfish at all times, people would tend to plod along, behaving equitably, in violation of their own self-interest."
They therefore offer

> PROPOSITION I: COROLLARY 1: So long as in-
> dividuals perceive they can maximize their outcomes
> by behaving equitably, they will do so. Should
> they perceive that they can maximize their outcomes
> by behaving inequitably, they will do so. [p. 16]

The coauthors expect a person who behaves inequitably to
feel badly, but for no more reason than that we are all
taught "that the man who dares to take too much, and gets

caught, can expect venomous retaliation; the man who ac-
cepts too little is not only deprived of material benefits,
but he may reap derision as well" (p. 17).

Cook and Messick (1983) note that while

> the earliest empirical research in equity theory fo-
> cused primarily upon reactions to pay inequities
> such as increased or decreased productivity or qual-
> ity of work, subsequent research effects extended
> the theory beyond wage inequities to apply it to the
> distribution of a wide range of valued outcomes.
> In addition, the theory was extended to a diverse
> set of social relationships and social situations, from
> business to intimate relations and from the work
> place to both the home and the society at large.
> [p. 2]

How valid research has been was questioned in 1982
by Homans, whose notion of distributive justice (Homans,
1961) is cited by McClintock and Keil (1982, p. 338) as the
beginning of the dominant definition of equity in social psychology. He protests that evidence is "largely from experi-
ments made on subjects enticed into university laboratories
and not from studies of 'real-life' situations carried on by
observation or interview" (p. xv). Disadvantages are that
it is often difficult to motivate subjects as strongly as they
are motivated in real life, and that subjects treated justly
and those treated unjustly may meet only once if at all, so
that some fundamental interactions, such as reprisals, are
not examined (pp. xv-xvi). Since this study is based on
interviews with librarians about real-life situations it should
be interesting to see how the findings compare with those
of the social psychologists.

Librarians were found during the interviews to relate
to directors, coworkers, friendly outside contacts, users,
and strangers in different ways. Walster et al. devote a
chapter to "Equity Theory and Intimate Relationships," stating that there is "some evidence that equity considerations
do seem to operate in close friendships and in romantic and
marital relationships" (p. 197). They see a difference between casual and intimate relationships, however, in that
strangers find even momentary inequities distressing, while
intimates do not (p. 161). Staub (1979) observes that in

continuing human relationships it is possible that a person
would act out of liking, loving or kindness, but still "return
benefits might be necessary to maintain the relationship"
(p. 373). Wilke (1983) adds the information that "subjects
who anticipated future interaction allocated more equally
(and less equitably) than did subjects who did not expect
future interaction" (p. 57).

A distinctive characteristic of Walster et al.'s equity
theory is the belief that the two major types of social justice
described by Aristotle, equal justice (rewards are distributed
equally) and proportional (that is, distributive) justice, are
identical, the difference being that in equal justice participants assume that the only relevant input is a person's
"humanity" (p. 214). Similarly, under a third type of social justice people's needs could be viewed as the only relevant input (p. 215).

Other authors feel that it is overreaching to try to
unify the three concepts into a single theory. A three-
fold distinction is commonly made. As Lerner and Meindl
(1981) state

> ... it has been pointed out that very often one can
> see a "Justice of Need" appear in the way parents
> allocate resources among family members. A "Justice
> of Equality" often dominates the relationship between
> friends, or those who want to maintain harmonious
> relations, whereas a justice based on the assessment
> of proportional contributions occurs most frequently
> in situations when there is an emphasis on produc-
> tivity--a work milieu. [p. 222]

The interviews with the librarians are in accord with
findings that dealings with strangers are based more on
equity than on equality or need. In general, librarians did
not express concern that restrictions on access to their own
collections would produce hardship for outsiders. They
were not governed by a concern for everyone's needs. In
some situations in which librarians expected to make some
use of another library they were generous to that library,
even if this meant that they gave significantly more than
they received. In these cases of expected future interaction, there was an appearance of equality, but the motivation
of being owed assistance in return was more in accord with

equity. If a library feared being overwhelmed by outsiders' requests, the rule of equity again was most likely to be applied. Librarians in smaller libraries facing restrictions on access to large research libraries sometimes felt that the larger library's dependence on its smaller neighbors was being underestimated, producing what they felt was an inequitable situation.

Whether or not librarians thought in terms of equity in dealing with outside personal contacts cannot be answered on the basis of the interviews. In doing favors for one another or in sharing confidences, librarians were engaged in a type of social exchange, but it is difficult to determine what part is played by liking and what by a calculated estimation of benefits.

Equity theory would cause us to expect librarians to shun relationships in which they cannot reciprocate favors. Walster et al. (1978) observe that the recipient of altruism "is in an unpleasant relationship for three different reasons: It is inequitable, potentially exploitative, and potentially humiliating" (p. 104). Staub (1978, p. 350) reports that research shows that people prefer conditions of reciprocity and dislike indebtedness and the people that are responsible for it, particularly when the need for help can be regarded as the consequence of personal inadequacy. The difficulty is summed up by Fisher and Nadler (1982) with an Indian proverb: "Why do you hate me--I've never helped you" (p. 131).

The interviews with librarians actually produced a mixture of attitudes towards accepting help without being able to offer help in return. When a long-term relationship with a nearby library existed, most librarians did not seem to want to receive much more than they gave, but librarians in smaller public libraries felt comfortable in being heavily dependent on their backup libraries. Apparently such a dependency was deemed logical and equitable. Librarians in one small public library were atypical in that they preferred to make referrals to a library that was not their assigned backup because they felt that their assigned backup library was inadequate. When instead of a long-term relationship librarians were involved in telephoning a place with which they had little or no previous interaction, there was except for a single instance no expression of concern

over making demands on outsiders. This finding is in accord with Walster et al.'s belief that equity is motivated in
part by a fear of retaliation.

While there is evidence that people behave equitably
and are under strong pressure to do so, Staub (1978) reports that "there is apparently a special consideration for
the self that keeps people from acting completely equitably"
(p. 188). Messick and Sentis (1983) found that subjects
selected as "fair" more money for themselves than for another
person in an identical situation, reflecting an "egocentric
bias" (p. 70). Some librarians' comments can be interpreted
in terms of such a bias, such as the tendency to find fault
with the library director, without admitting that the director's approach may have some justification. At the same
time, the directors indeed may have been mistreating their
subordinates due to an egocentric bias of their own. Hollander (1980) notes that in social exchange terms the leader's demands upon the followers are reciprocated in demands
made upon the leader. Therefore, "the integrity of the relationship depends upon some yielding to influence on both
sides" (p. 107).

Related to the concept of egocentric bias is the concept of ethnocentric bias, an example of which is the tendency of spectators at a football game to feel that the other
side was guilty of more fouls (Messick and Sentis, 1983,
pp. 82-84). Similarly librarians were more likely to think
that other libraries took unfair advantage of them than they
were to think that they took unfair advantage of others.
Rabbie (1982, p. 123) notes that experimental research on
intergroup relations is relatively sparse, in part because it
is very difficult to create intergroup relations in the laboratory. In what Nord (1980) describes as "their famous paper on interorganizational exchange" (p. 123), Levine and
White (1961) explained that "domain consensus," the clarification of organizational domains, is necessary to competing
community health and welfare agencies for determining "who
gets what and for what purpose" (p. 599). They specifically
mention referrals as one of the major elements exchanged by
these organizations (p. 589).

Besides dealing with outside institutions and with their
own directors, librarians interviewed exhibited a consciousness of equity in dealing with users. Some users, especially

students, were thought by some librarians to have too little
motivation to deserve much assistance. The librarian
identified as the Exemplary Referrer was found to interpret
an apparent lack of interest as possibly due to feelings of
inferiority, which the librarian ought to help the user overcome. Bar-Tal (1976) makes a relevant observation concerning the decision whether to help someone:

> ... the person may judge that the other is in need
> because he is lazy and therefore it is not rewarding
> to help him. Or the person may judge that it is
> very costly to help the other in terms of effort and
> therefore may rationalize that the other is in need
> because of laziness. [p. 56]

Such a rationalization is what Walster et al. (1978) would
call "restoring psychological equity" by convincing one's
self that an inequitable relationship is, in fact, equitable
(p. 28). The inequity would be the inadequate assistance
given the user, at least in terms of a sympathetic level of
service.

Walster et al. note that "theorists have observed that
people possess an intense need to perceive this as a fair
and equitable world, a world where both the enormously
benefited and the under benefited deserve their fates" (p.
220). "An impressive body of research" by Melvin J. Lerner
has documented this point, they state (p. 220). They cite
several ways in which harmdoers distort reality: blaming
the victim, minimization of the victim's suffering, or denial
of responsibility for the victim's suffering (p. 30).

Some instances of librarians interviewed derogating
users could have been examples of blaming the victim, making the user responsible for an inadequate reference encounter. Statements that users, especially students, did not require much referral could have been examples of minimization
of suffering, making it appear that inadequate referral service produced no real hardship. Librarians who exhibited
little or no concern over making frequent demands on libraries that were not reimbursed for such service also may
have been exhibiting a minimization technique.

So far this review has concentrated on equity. Messick
and Sentis (1983) observe:

> Social comparison processes are not the only proc-
> esses that cause our satisfaction to depend upon
> the outcomes that others receive. Another impor-
> tant process is empathetic responding to others'
> outcomes. Empathetic responding means feeling
> vicariously the pleasure or pain or the satisfaction
> or dissatisfaction of another person. [p. 67]

These authors believe that helping another person with whom
one is empathetically linked can be considered to be hedon-
istic, since one's own satisfaction is augmented by increases
in another's satisfaction. The question of whether empathy
or even altruism is motivated by self-gratification will be
returned to later. The point to be examined first is to
what extent empathy influences behavior.

The view that affect, sympathetic or empathetic, is
present in prosocial activity "seems to be fairly well documented," Rosenhan (1978, p. 106) claims. Hoffman (1982,
p. 294) states, however, that people may employ certain
techniques to reduce empathy that is too distressing. These
include avoiding people in pain, or derogating victims such
as by making negative attributions about their motives or
blaming them for their plights. Feshback (1982) concludes:
"Whereas we expect empathy to contribute to and facilitate
prosocial behaviors, the relationship will inevitably be at-
tenuated and complex" (p. 336).

The overall impression from the interviews with the
librarians was that of a concern for equity not empathy,
but empathy was not totally absent. Indications of empathy
included the Exemplary Referrer's satisfaction in seeing
awareness come to the hesitant student, and another librarian's preference for helping people who seemed the most
confused. Perhaps interviewees felt that discussing their
empathic feelings would be embarrassing. It may be that
such feelings toward users are common. Staub (1978)
suggests that "helping a person in certain kinds of need
may be a safe form of approach and affiliation with others"
(p. 306). Empathy is probably also present in the generally
positive regard expressed for coworkers, and in the friendships with employees of other libraries.

The fact that the female librarians interviewed were
more likely to report that they themselves received feedback
suggests that they may have had greater rapport with users,

possibly due in part to their having more empathy. Females
also were more likely to express empathic regard for users.
However, it was not found that women in general were less
judgmental in dealing with users and outsiders, or less critical of directors. Equity seemed to be the prevailing mode
of thought for both sexes.

The idea that women are more empathetic than men has
received wide support. Walster et al. (1978) write that
evidence for the "contention that males are more exploitative
than females comes from a number of studies" (p. 212).
Fisher, DePaulo and Nadler (1981) conclude from a literature
review that "females appear to be more comfortable with
helping relationships than males...." (p. 405). Deutsch
(1982) contends that the "equity system"

> is associated with an economic mode of thought that
> is characterized by quantification, measurement,
> calculation, comparison, evaluation, impersonality,
> and conversion of unique values to a common cur-
> rency. It is a cool, detached, future-oriented, an-
> alytic, tough-minded mode of thought that appeals
> to universalistic values, logical reasoning, and ob-
> jective reality rather than particularistic values,
> intuition, emotion, and subjective considerations.
> It is more prevalent in men than in women. (p.
> 39)

More prevalent among women, Deutsch states, is the "equality system," associated with a particularistic, social-
emotional orientation that is characterized by reliance on
intuition, empathy, and powerful feeling as a guide to reality. Staub (1978, p. 232) also concludes that males are
more concerned with equity than equality, and tend to
maximize their own equity in comparison to females. Similarly, Major and Deaux (1982) report that when women's inputs
are greater than their partners', "women appear to follow a
norm of equality, whereas men appear to follow a norm of
equity" (p. 51).

In contrast to these findings and opinions, Eisenberg
and Lennon (1983) reached the following conclusions:

> It is clear from the review of the empirical literature
> that the data regarding sex differences in empathy

are inconsistent, and that this inconsistency is a
function of the method used to measure empathy.
Sex differences in empathy favoring females are
most evident when individuals have been asked to
rate themselves on behaviors or affective responses
related to the concept of empathy and/or sympathy.
Somewhat weaker sex differences favoring females
have been found when subjects have been asked to
rate their emotional responses in contrived situations
or in response to hypothetical picture/story measures. In contrast, few consistent sex differences
in empathy have been noted in research in which
empathy was assessed with physiological measures
and/or facial/gestural measures.... [p. 124]

Since "emotionality and nuturance are both part of the
stereotypic feminine role," Eisenberg and Lennon think that
"it is highly likely that females would be more willing than
males to present themselves as being empathic and/or sympathetic, even if there were not real sex difference in responsiveness" (p. 125).

In introducing the topic of empathy the question was
raised whether people ever act from purely selfless motives.
Blau (1964) writes, "Professionals are expected to be governed in their work exclusively by professional standards of
performance and conduct not by consideration of exchange
with clients" (p. 261). Are such normative standards ad-
hered to because society's rules of equity demand it, as
Walster et al. would claim, or can concern for others' welfare
be the principal motive?

Darley and Latané (1970) state that "altruistic behavior
may please us as people, but it embarrasses traditional theories of psychology that are founded on the assumption that
man is moved only by considerations of reinforcement" (p.
83). They observe that upholders of reinforcement theory
argue that altruistic acts relieve the actor's sympathetic
distress or are examples of adhering to norms that the actor
must follow to avoid punishment. Hoffman (1981) agrees that
"the doctrinaire view in psychology has long been that altrui-
ism can ultimately be explained in terms of egoistic, self-
serving motives" (p. 41). He argues, however, that because
people have a satisfied feeling after helping someone does
not necessarily mean that they acted in order to have such
a feeling (p. 55).

Rushton (1981) states that "the only major researcher who approaches the conclusion that there is an altruistic personality is Ervin Staub," who "has suggested that people differ in the degree to which they have a general 'prosocial orientation'" (p. 252). Staub (1978, p. 111) himself admits that the question of whether helpful conduct is "selfish" is more ideological or philosophical than empirical. He observes that a number of psychological conceptions of human nature seem to be related to earlier, philosophical ones (p. 10). The notion that human nature has within it the elements of human goodness traces back to Plato (pp. 13-14), and the assumption that humans are inherently evil has been long present in philosophy, especially in the work of Thomas Hobbes (p. 17). David Hume

> was one of the foremost expositors of the view that man's selfish motives could lead to the development of a positive social order. Self-love, he thought, would give rise to justice and greed would give rise to honesty because of man's ability to judge that in the long run the practice of such virtues would bring him more gratification than a more direct expression of his passions. [p. 21]

The enlightened self-interest discussed by Hume is reflected in Staub's observation that

> the greater the cost of helping--the amount of sacrifice, the social courage required--the less likely may be a decision to help or actual helping. This is generally assumed to be true and is supported by the existing data. However, to satisfactorily consider the significance of costs the nature and type of connection that exists between the self and others, the degree of interrelatedness that people perceive to exist between another person or persons and themselves, must be considered. People may identify with others to such an extent that their own interests and those of the other person are considered identical. Under such (presumably rare) circumstances, will people still help less if the costs of helping are greater? More frequently, the interests of the self and of others are interrelated but not identical. [p. 427]

The librarian may decide to be especially considerate

of the user, or may be particularly generous to the outside
user, out of a belief that spreading knowledge will make a
better society for all, but this degree of enlightened self-
interest will in many cases seem farfetched. To examine
another type of motivation, related to the Platonic view of
human nature as being morally good, attention will be given
next to an author whom Staub associates with this view,
Lawrence Kohlberg.

THE FAITH OF LAWRENCE KOHLBERG

Staub (1979) has stated that both philosophers and
psychologists have entertained each of the following three
conceptions: "that human beings are basically 'bad,' meaning that they are selfish and only concerned about their
own welfare...; that human beings are basically good or
have the potential to be good...; and, finally, that the
conditions of man living in a social group can lead to enlightened self-interest, to an understanding that one's interests and the interests of others are interrelated, and
that cooperation and mutual help are needed to live har-
moniously with others" (p. 4). This last view assumes that
"human nature is neither basically good nor bad but that
man has the potential for developing optimal social characteristics" (p. 5). Staub (1978, p. 24) places social exchange
theory under the enlightened self-interest approach, but
Walster et al.'s version of exchange theory, with its emphasis on people's selfishness, seems to fit better the "people
are bad" concept. It is the observation of this study that
librarians generally seemed to fit one or the other of these
latter two notions. To complete the analysis, an examination
will now be made of how well the librarians interviewed reflect the "people are good" idea.

Staub (1978) cites Rogers, Maslow, and Fromm as examples of contemporary psychologists who have implied that
human nature is good or that people will become good under
the right circumstances. He believes that "their writing
represents a social philosophy or psychological humanitarian-
ism, that has little scientific support as yet" (p. 16). The
only other modern theorist cited by Staub as assuming that
humans are morally good is the "currently influential" Kohlberg, who reports empirical evidence that people progres-
sively evolve higher levels of morality, not through direct

instruction or inculcation of tradition but simply through
experiencing varied roles in interaction with other people
(p. 17).

Kohlberg has conducted his research by asking his
subjects to make decisions regarding a set of hypothetical
dilemmas that pose conflicts between the rights or claims of
different persons. The questions posed have sought to
probe his subjects' reasoning, with the focus on issues of
rightness and justice. Building upon the work of Jean
Piaget, Kohlberg has identified seven stages of development.
He stresses, "I have always tried to be clear that my stages
are stages of justice reasoning, not of emotions, aspirations,
or action" (1984, p. 224).

Stage 1

defines the "sociomoral order" in terms of differen-
tials of power status and possessions, rather than
in terms of equality or reciprocity. The "principles"
maintaining the social order are obedience by the
weak to the strong and punishment by the strong
of those who deviate. [1981, p. 148]

Does this stage apply to any of the library situations disclosed in the interviews? Some librarians who were experiencing conflict with their library directors seemed to consider
themselves the victims of Stage 1 thinking. Similarly, librarians angered by restrictive access policies at other libraries may have felt like victims of Stage 1 attitudes.

In Stage 2, there is "an emphasis on instrumental exchange as a mechanism through which individuals can coor-
dinate their actions for mutual benefit" (1984, p. 626). An
important limitation of Stage 2 is that "it fails to provide a
means for deciding among conflicting claims, ordering or
setting priorities on conflicting needs and interests." Norms
"have no fixed values except insofar as they allow individuals
to have expectations of one another which maintain a balance
through exchange." Krebs (1978) concludes that at Stage 2,
"altruism is rooted in the idea of helping those who help
you" (p. 153). Stage 2 is considered to be a childish level
of development, and it is unlikely that any of the librarians
interviewed were operating primarily on such a simplistic
level.

Stage 3, generally reached in late elementary school, is thought to be characteristic of a sizable portion of the adult population (Krebs, 1978, p. 153). In Stage 3, "reciprocity involves the notions of obligation, debt, and gratitude which allow one to understand reciprocity as giving beyond concrete notions of equal exchange to maintaining relationships, mutuality of expectations, and sentiments of gratitude and obligation" (1984, p. 629). Stage 3 norms emphasize "being a good, altruistic, or prosocial role occupant...." (p. 628). Krebs (1982) observes that

> although the principles of justice that evolve during the first three stages of moral development become increasingly conducive to "altruistic behavior," this conduciveness may well peak at Kohlberg's Stage 3. The principles that evolve after that prescribe an increasing attentiveness to the larger social context, sometimes in a way that is inconsistent with generosity towards individuals. For example, at Stage 3 people might give money to a beggar because they feel sorry for him, but at later stages they may refuse to give because they believe that such "generosity" is ultimately destructive to the social system that they (and the beggar) have an obligation to preserve. [pp. 301-302]

With four stages yet to be described, Stage 3 would not seem to be a very high level of moral development. This point has been contested, however, as will be discussed later. A more immediate question is whether Stage 3 fits the librarians interviewed. With its emphasis on prosocial behavior it might be expected to. Reference work is prosocial, meaning that it is behavior that benefits other people. The regard some librarians felt for their coworkers may have been an example of Stage 3, with the librarian who said that he would not correct a coworker in front of a user for fear of embarrassing his coworker being an example of Stage 3 excessive kindness. Some might argue that the several librarians who admitted to violating policies of their or another library in order to assist someone were also exhibiting Stage 3 excess. In general, however, Stage 3 reasoning did not seem to be predominant.

At Stage 4,

the individual takes the perspective of a generalized
member of society. This perspective is based on a
conception of the social system as a consistent set
of codes and procedures that apply impartially to all
members. [Kohlberg, 1984, p. 631]

The perspective taken is "generally that of a societal, legal,
or religious system which has been codified into institutional
laws and practices" (p. 631). The attitude prevails that
"one should obey the law because respect for the law will
be destroyed if citizens feel they can break it just because
they disagree with it" (p. 633). Generally, in Stage 4,

maintaining respect for property rights as a return
for investment of effort is considered to be central
to social organization. On the other hand, property
rights may be seen as contingent upon demonstration
of social responsibility. [p. 633]

Stage 4 seems to best fit the librarians interviewed.
Librarians accepted their own institutions' strictures on
service to outsiders almost without exception. As regards
restrictions imposed by outside institutions, both Stage 4
positions regarding property rights were represented: that
libraries had the right to restrict access and, alternatively,
that such restrictions were not socially responsibile. Interactions with users seemed to be largely governed by expectations of "proper" behavior on their part. Interactions
with coworkers and with directors could also be interpreted
in terms of meeting generally held expectations.

Stage 5 is a "prior-to-society perspective,"

that of a rational moral agent aware of universalizable
values and rights that anyone would choose to build
into a moral society. The validity of actual laws and
social systems can be evaluated in terms of the degree to which they preserve and protect these fundamental human rights and values. [p. 634]

Within the Stage 5 perspective, the primary focus is either
on rights or on social welfare. In the former orientation

each person has an obligation to make moral choices
that uphold these rights, even when they conflict

> with society's laws or codes. There is a concern
> for the protection of the rights of the minority that
> cannot be derived from the social system perspective
> of Stage 4. [p. 634]

The social welfare orientation "reflects a rule-utilitarian
philosophy in which social institutions, rules, or laws are
evaluated by reference to their long-term consequences for
the welfare of each person or group in the society" (p.
634).

It is not possible to fully categorize librarians interviewed as Stage 5 versus Stage 4 because an individual who
appeared to be acquiescent in accepting all policies and
practices may have had more considered reasons for appearing so than simply blind obedience. Still, some tentative
conclusions can be drawn.

Regarding other libraries' restrictions on outsiders'
access, several librarians appeared to present access to information as a fundamental human right that was being
abridged. Their observations were at least somewhat self-
serving, however, since the restrictions were likely to com-
plicate these librarians' ability to serve their own primary
clientele. A few librarians defended such restrictions on
access as upholding the rights of the restrictive institutions.
In some cases this may have been due to a Stage 4 compli-
ance with the status quo, but there were expressions of
concern about unfairly overloading the restrictive libraries,
which could indicate concern over fundamental rights or
long-term social consequences. Concerning their own service to outsiders, librarians with few exceptions seemed to
be more clearly at Stage 4, doing what they were obligated
to do, or even Stage 2, thinking of it as a simple reciprocal
arrangement.

Service to primary users is a complex issue. A few
librarians mentioned adhering to a philosophy of equal service, but this appeared to be more a Stage 4 reference to a
societal norm, with actual practice drawing many distinctions.
Giving more service to a higher status user can be a Stage
5 practice if it is done because it is felt that these people
contribute more to society and therefore society benefits
more when they are served, although such a belief would be
objected to vigorously by other Stage 5 reasoners.

As regards feedback, at Stage 5 there should have
been some interest in organized feedback to protect users'
rights, or to improve society through better library service.
For the same reasons Stage 5 should require ability to give
directions to likely places of referral, rather than the widespread inability discovered. In describing the safest way
to visit inner-city libraries, several librarians could be said
to have shown a Stage 5 disregard for social sanctions
against broaching a delicate subject.

In their relations with their directors, librarians were
mainly noncommittal or, in a sizable minority of cases, adversely critical. At a Stage 5 level a broader perspective
should probably be evident, with more appreciation or at
least understanding expressed of the director's point of
view.

Dealings with coworkers do not raise as many Stage 5
issues. Relations seemed pleasant in a functional Stage 4
sense or in a more personal Stage 3 fashion. The occasional
criticism of or disregard of nonprofessional coworkers seemed
a bit harsh for Stage 5, which would require some understanding from the nonprofessional's point of view.

In summary, there were few obvious Stage 5 responses.
There was concern among many librarians about making unreasonable demands on other libraries. Some of this concern
could have been due to a Stage 2 fear of retaliation, or a
Stage 4 allegiance to established property rights, but some
seemed to be due to a reasoned understanding that outside
librarians are busy and have limited resources. Similarly,
advising a user about safe travel to a library in a high-
crime area could be merely a reflection of a Stage 4 adher-
ence to local prejudices, but if done in an area where the
prevailing opinion is that it is safest for the librarian not
to raise such topics, it can reflect a Stage 5 concern for the
welfare of others.

The possibility that people may use one level of moral
reasoning in one situation and another level in another situation is recognized in the literature. Mischel and Mischel
(1976, p. 88) contend that Kohlberg's theory does not permit one to separate the type of moral reasoning of which the
respondent is capable from the moral reasoning that he favors
in a particular situation.

Kohlberg's Stage 6 "is not so much 'based' on a new social perspective beyond Stage 5's notion of a prior-to-society perspective as it is on a <u>deliberate</u> use of the justice operations as principles to ensure that perspective when reasoning about normal dilemmas" (Kohlberg, 1984, p. 318). Justice is grounded in the principles of universalizability and reversibility (p. 317). At this stage,

> equity does not include reference to special rewards for talent, merit, or achievement. These are largely seen as resulting from differences in genes or in educational and social opportunities which are morally arbitrary, or to unequal distribution by society. However, Stage 6 equity does include recognition of differential need, that is the need to consider the position of the least advantaged. Where distribution of scarce basic goods must be unequal (e.g., issues of who should live in "life-boat" dilemmas) a lottery approach is preferred to favoring the strong or more socially useful. [p. 638]

Kohlberg makes justice rather than love the central principle at Stage 6 because "love involves us in the realm of supererogation, not duties on which all could agree" (p. 484). However, he makes a major concession to critics who have accused him of being too little concerned with caring:

> ... at the postconventional stages there is typically an effort to integrate concerns of benevolence and care, on the one hand, with justice concerns, on the other. At this level of moral reasoning, justice concerns lose their retributive and rule-bound nature for the sake of treating persons as persons, that is, as ends in themselves. This principle of persons as ends is common to both the ethic of care and the ethic of justice. The former ethic sees the other person in relationship to self and others; the latter sees persons as autonomous ends in themselves, relating to one another through agreement and mutual respect. [p. 356]

Stage 6's concept of equity, with distribution based on need rather than achievement, is not very characteristic of the librarians interviewed. Several expressions of regret that some users are denied access to private research

libraries may touch on this stage. Kohlberg himself con-
cedes that Stage 6 is speculative, unlike his claims for
Stage 5, which he says are demonstrable (p. 274).

Of Kohlberg's Stage 7 little need be said. It is a
postulation of a "soft" stage of ethical awareness, with "an
orientation based on ethical and religious thinking involving
a cosmic or religious perspective on life" (p. 213). He
adds that "this soft stage is not a strictly moral one, nor
do we intend that it be understood as a hard stage of justice reasoning constructed beyond Stage 6." Hard structural
stage models "define structures in a way consistent with the
Piagetian construction of structure, that is, as an organization of manifest thought operations" (p. 244).

If Kohlberg's higher stages seem vague or overly
idealistic, there are alternatives to both his concept of moral
development and the earlier discussed equity theory, which
seems to fall at Stage 2 or Stage 4 in his analysis. One
alternative, to be considered next, might be described as
a defense of life at his Stage 3.

AN ALTERNATIVE: CARING

The alternative to Kohlberg considered here is one
addressed by Kohlberg himself. It is the approach of Carol
Gilligan, whose In a Different Voice: Psychological Theory
and Women's Development he discusses in his The Psychology
of Moral Development (1984). Also considered here is Nel
Noddings' Caring: A Feminine Approach to Ethics and Moral
Education, which was published too late to be discussed in
Kohlberg's book but which is similar to Gilligan's work.

Based on interviews that explored conceptions about
self, morality, conflict, and choice, Gilligan concluded that
women view morality as "arising from the experience of connection and conceived as a problem of inclusion rather than
one of balancing claims" so that "morality stems from attachment" (p. 160).

Noddings states that Kohlberg's theory "is widely held
to be a model for moral education, but it is actually only a
hierarchical description of moral reasoning" (pp. 95-96).
She continues:

It is well known, further, that the description may
not be accurate. In particular, the fact that women
seem often to be "stuck" at stage three might call
the accuracy of the description into question. But
perhaps the description is accurate within the domain of morality conceived as moral justification. If
it is, we might well explore the possibility that
feminine nonconformity to the Kohlberg model counts
against the justification/judgment paradigm and not
against women as moral thinkers. [p. 96]

Noddings believes that the ethical ideal

springs from two sentiments: the natural sympathy
human beings feel for each other and the longing to
maintain, recapture, or enhance our most caring and
tender moments. [p. 104]

In a statement that could be taken as a challenge to reli-
giously minded people, Kohlberg, and the social psychological equity theorists, she adds:

There are those who locate the source of their ethi-
cality in god, and others who find theirs in reason,
and still others who find theirs in self-interest. I
am certainly not denying the existence of these
positions nor their power to motivate some individuals, but I am suggesting that they do not ring true
to many of us and that they seem off the mark or
unnecessarily cumbersome in their search for justification. [p. 104]

Noddings acknowledges: "Our ethic of caring--which
we might have called a 'feminine ethic'--begins to look a bit
mean in contrast to the masculine ethics of universal love or
universal justice." However, "universal love is illusion"
(p. 90). Gilligan's woman examines conventions of "female
self-abnegation and moral self-sacrifice" (p. 90), questioning
"not only the justification for hurting others in the name of
morality but also the 'rightness' of hurting herself" (p. 87).

Considering that female librarians predominated in the
interviews in this study, the claim that women's moral development differs from that of men is of interest. However,
the only relevant discovery during the interviews was that

a few of the female librarians seemed to have more rapport
with users, judging from their reports of more feedback,
their expression of more empathy, and their perhaps having
more pleasant personalities.

Kohlberg himself believes that "dilemmas located within
a 'community' or 'family' context are likely to invoke caring
and response considerations." In brief, choice of orientation
between justice and caring "seems to be primarily a function
of setting and dilemma, not sex." He contends that many
women properly do not define or select special relationship
dilemmas as moral (1984, p. 350).

Kohlberg states that a literature review of "studies
comparing the sexes in justice reasoning either report no
sex differences or report sex differences attributable to
higher education and role-taking opportunity differences
related to work" (p. 358). He attests, "I have never directly stated that males have a more developed sense of
justice than do females." Rather, he continues,

> I suggested that if women were not provided with
> the experience of participation in society's complex
> secondary institutions through education and complex
> work responsibility, then they were not likely to
> acquire those societal role-taking abilities necessary
> for the development of Stage 4 and 5 justice reason-
> ing. [p. 340]

Work experience "with a certain level of moral complexity
requires a person simultaneously to take the perspective of
individuals within a system and of the system as a whole,"
and "this experience aids development to principled thinking"
(p. 468). Thus Kohlberg would not expect male and female
librarians to differ in reasoning regarding equity.

More than Gilligan, Noddings expects caring to involve
sacrifice, especially when assisting those "who came to me
without the bonds established in my chains of caring" (p.
47). She observes that to avoid being "bombarded with
stimuli that arouse the 'I must,'" strangers may be reacted
to with situational rules. By relying too much on external
rules, however, "I become detached from the very heart of
morality: the sensibility that calls forth caring: (p. 47).
The caring person

> dreads the proximate stranger, for she cannot easily
> reject the claim he has on her. She would prefer
> that the stray cat not appear at the back door--or
> the stray teenager at the front. But if either pre-
> sents himself, he must be received not by formula
> but as individual. [p. 47]

Noddings' challenge to Kohlberg is that

> today we are asked to believe that women's "lack of
> experience in the world" keeps them at an inferior
> stage in moral development. I am suggesting, to
> the contrary, that a powerful and coherent ethic and,
> indeed, a different sort of world may be built on the
> natural caring so familiar to women. [p. 46]

Yet Noddings and Kohlberg do not really seem to be so far
apart, since Kohlberg's Stage 6 equity requirements, as
presented earlier, would also appear to demand that the
needy stranger be helped.

The finding of this study is that librarians interviewed
saw service to the stranger or outsider more as a debt or a
payment in an equity relationship, either in relation to particular outside institutions or to society in general. This
is not to deny that there is the type of attachment or caring
described by Gilligan or Noddings. The Exemplary Referrer's
expression of concern for the unenlightened student, and
delight when the student begins to show comprehension, are
mirrored in a comment by Noddings: "What the cared-for
gives to the relation either in direct response to the one-
caring or in personal delight or in happy growth before her
eyes is genuine reciprocity" (p. 74).

This satisfaction achieved by the one-caring recalls
the debate in the psychological literature regarding the nature of altruism. There, too, there was recognition that
service to others, even if altruistic in the sense of not consciously being done to achieve self-gain, cannot be entirely
separated from eventual reward. In a related observation,
Kohlberg states that "many of the classical arguments for
Stage 5 moralities are social contract arguments designed to
show that commitment to social law is the best strategy for
Stage 2 instrumentally egoistic people" (1981, p. 156).

There are clear advantages to one's self in behaving positively toward coworkers, one's director, and the users one is obligated to serve. The advantage to self in assisting the user of a library from which one expects no favors in return is not so obvious. Outside of the possible inner satisfaction of having behaved in a caring way, extending one's self to outsiders may be against the policy of one's own library and may threaten to leave too little time and resources to assist one's primary clientele.

The philosopher MacIntyre (1984) describes a time and a place in which the conflict between one's own and another's interests was less likely to occur: the ancient Greek city-state. In such a close-knit community, what was good for a fellow citizen was, according to Aristotle, good for one's self. MacIntyre states:

> It was in the seventeenth and eighteenth centuries that morality came generally to be understood as offering a solution to the problems posed by human egoism and that the content of morality came to be largely equated with altruism. For it was in that same period that men came to be thought of as in some dangerous measure egoistic by nature; and it is only once we think of mankind as by nature dangerously egoistic that altruism becomes at once socially necessary and yet apparently impossible and, if and when it occurs, inexplicable. On the traditional Aristotelian view such problems do not arise. For what education in the virtues teaches me is that my good as a man is one and the same as the good of those others with whom I am bound up in human community. [pp. 228-229]

For MacIntyre, only in the type of community known to Aristotle can there be a resolution of the conflict found between the present-day philosophical positions of Robert Nozick and John Rawls. Nozick claims, in MacIntyre's words, that if the world were wholly just "the only people entitled to hold anything, that is to appropriate it for use as they and they alone wished, would be those who had justly acquired what they held by some just act of original acquisition and those who had justly acquired what they held by some just act of transfer from someone else who had either acquired it by some just act of original acquisition or by

some just transfer ... and so on" (p. 247). Rawls, Mac-
Intyre points out, "makes primary what is in effect a principle of equality with respect to entitlement" (p. 248). For
Rawls, "how those who are now in grave need came to be
in grave need is irrelevant; justice is made into a matter
of present patterns of distribution to which the past is
irrelevant" (p. 248).

Rawls' position is similar to Kohlberg's Stage 6 and
Noddings' acceptance of the needy stranger. Nozick's emphasis on the rights of individual owners is closer to most
psychological theories of equity and to the practice and beliefs of the librarians interviewed. For MacIntyre the conflict of interests in today's complex society has created "a
new dark age" (p. 263).

CONCLUSION

The results of this study's exploration of referral
seem to indicate that primary concerns in making referrals
are efficiency and equity, with equity being the more complicated decision process. A review of the literature of social psychology regarding equity provides support for the
belief that people are governed by an equity based on self-
gain, that is, maximizing personal outcomes, and this description seems to fit the librarians interviewed.

Kohlberg offers as an alternative theory that people
progress to higher stages of moral development, ideally
reaching a stage at which they generously make distributions
according to perceived needs of the receiver, not according
to perceived contributions of the receiver. Conversations
with librarians did not indicate that they were functioning
at this level.

Noddings calls for a similar generosity, although she
does not base her argument on a theory of justice, as does
Kohlberg, but rather on an ethic of caring. Caring, for
her, has a reciprocal aspect, so that self-gain is still acknowledged. Kohlberg, too, would allow that acting in an
altruistic manner may provide some emotional or other benefit for the giver.

The greatest challenge seems to be in deciding whether

to help the outsider when there is little if any likelihood of receiving help in return, and when there is no other strong motivator such as to avoid guilt or to protect a firmly held belief in equal access to information.

CHAPTER 5

SUMMARY AND CONCLUSIONS

OVERVIEW

This book began with a desire to understand the factors that influence the referral process in libraries. Why one librarian would be enthusiastic and skillful in making referrals and another librarian would be reluctant and unskilled was expected to relate to a number of factors internal to librarians, such as their attitudes and beliefs, and a number of factors relating to their libraries and to outside institutions. Since the subject had not been well explored, it was decided not to hypothesize about which factors were most important and then attempt to measure them. Rather it was decided to see which ones emerged from an extensive analysis of interviews with librarians on a broad range of topics concerning their experiences with and attitudes about referral.

This analysis resulted in the description of a variety of factors: the personal qualities of equity, empathy, tact, efficiency, achievement motivation, and independence; factors centering on the librarian's own library and relating to the directors, coworkers, training and experience, the activity level at the reference desk, collection strength, and referral aids; factors centering on outside resources and relating to availability and knowledge of these resources, relations with

136

outsiders, and interaction with faculty; and the client-
centered factors of evaluating, cautioning, and obtaining
feedback from users. Referral itself was defined function-
ally as "an act by library employees of responding to individuals' needs by directing these individuals to another
person, or to a place under the control of another person,
for the fulfillment of these needs."

EQUITY AND REFERRAL

A key concept that seemed to influence much of what
happened in library referral was discovered. That concept
was the notion of equity as described by McClintock and Keil
(1982) and others, the concern that people (in this case
library users and librarians) get what they deserve. For
most social psychologists, "equity" has the more specific
meaning that what people receive should be proportional to
what they contribute to the interaction or to the system.
Called also the "contributions rule" (Leventhal, 1980, p.
30), this was the predominant type of equity found in library referral. Contributions may be described as "economic," meaning related to the cost of the work done meas-
ured in time or money; or "social," related either to status
in the community or to positive interpersonal qualities, such
as friendliness or attentiveness.

Two other types of equity pertaining to library referral are described in the literature and help to a lesser extent to explain the data: the "equality rule," under which
both sides have an equal right to profit from a relationship
regardless of contributions; and the "needs rule," by which
one side is only expected to contribute and the other side
is only expected to receive. The term "equity" in this final
chapter is used in the broader sense of including the contributions, equality, and needs rules.

The literature reviewed suggests three perspectives
that may be posited as interacting with equity: self-interest,
idealism, and empathy. Self-interest requires that people
consider whether they are benefiting from a relationship.
It is similar to the equity perspective of social psychologists
such as Walster et al., who believe that people strive only
to benefit themselves. Idealism applies a general principle
to protect the rights of others and is found in Kohlberg's

fifth and sixth stages of moral development. Empathy, more recently represented by the writings of Gilligan and Noddings, shows a concern for the welfare of others based on feeling and caring. While Noddings does approach a general principle in her call for assistance to strangers, and Kohlberg does not deny the role of empathy, the emphasis in Noddings' writings is on feelings and in Kohlberg on a rational moral argument.

The perspective of self-interest complicates those of empathy and idealism. Personal satisfaction can be taken in feelings of empathy. Similarly, while following Kohlberg's Stage 5 and Stage 6 moral ideals may be done primarily for the good of others, there are often related self-rewarding aspects, such as feeling good about oneself; or rewards from others, such as being considered a worthy person. Altruistic behavior, then, can be considered unselfish in that it is not primarily motivated by the desire for personal gain, but there is frequently such gain associated with it.

Self interest also complicates the notion of equity. A primarily self-interested orientation may be present even in the person who upholds equality despite making the larger contribution in an interaction, or who upholds the needs rule despite having to contribute to someone who does not contribute in return. The self-interest in these instances can be in terms such as feeling superior or enjoying the security of being owed rather than being in debt.

The findings of this study are that the contributions, equality, and needs rules fit the equity relationships described by librarians interviewed about referral and that, while the contributions rule motivated by self-interest predominates, some indication of motivation by empathy and idealism was found also in these interactions. As to what extent self-interest may influence empathy and idealism in the referral process, that question can best be answered after describing the major equity relationships as they relate to the process portrayed by librarians interviewed.

Perhaps most basic to the study of referral are relationships with other libraries. Here the contributions rule was predominant. Librarians did not, and from a practical viewpoint could not, expect an exact balance between what they gave to and what they received from other libraries.

However, they gave much attention to gauging the extent
of imbalance. In general, they seemed to avoid asking
significantly more favors than they received from another
library, except in a few cases in which the other library
was felt to be obligated to assist outsiders or at least encouraged use by outsiders. On the other hand, providing
somewhat more unfunded service than was received in return was considered to be a favorable proportion in that
one was thereby owed assistance. In form this may appear
to be an example of the equality rule, but in spirit it follows the contributions rule because the imbalance in contributions relative to gains in the other party's favor is viewed
as benefiting oneself by providing insurance of help when
needed. Finally, giving or being in danger of giving much
more unreimbursed help to outsiders than can be received
in return seemed to be widely avoided. There was not
idealism or empathy enough for have-nots to excuse such
cost.

Also found to be of great importance in the referral
transaction is the attitude towards the user. What is perhaps surprising here is that there is again a frequent application of the contributions rule even though, unless the
librarian is dealing with an outside user, there is payment
for services in that the library is funded to provide reference and referral service. As applied to the user, the
contributions rule has both economic and social aspects.
In economic terms, the librarian is likely to object if the
user makes too great a demand for service. In social
terms, the librarian expects interest and respect from the
user and is also likely to be affected in the referral process
by the user's status.

Unlike dealings with other libraries, however, equity
judgments about users for many librarians seem to be affected not only by self-interest but also by idealism or empathy. The ideal of impartial service to all mitigates the
effect of the contributions rule to some extent. In addition,
the most insightful and helpful service seemed to be influenced by empathy, as exemplified by the Exemplary Referrer,
who not only gave evidence of a very broad knowledge of
outside resources, but who also sought to reach the inse-
cure student who displayed a facade of indifference. This
librarian applies the needs rule: she still extends the best
possible service even if the user remains passive. This is

not to deny the possibility of gain for the librarian. There
is the hope of reaching the student, which brings empathetic
satisfaction like that received by the one-caring from the
cared for in Noddings' description (page 132 above).

Occasionally the librarian must turn to a coworker for
assistance, including referral information. A key aspect
here may be the occasional nature of the interaction. Librarians did not appear to be so dependent on coworkers
for aid that a sense of being overly dependent or for the
coworkers, overused, would develop. Also, providing coworkers with suggestions when asked is, of course, considered to be part of one's normal job duties. The operating
principle seems to be the equality rule, with no great concern about the ratio of contributions. Exchanges are mainly
social; in fact, sociability is quite important for these librarians who must interact on a daily basis. Empathy is
sometimes, perhaps frequently, present. However, a different relationship sometimes applies to nonprofessional coworkers, due to their lower status or to concern about their
providing users with incorrect information.

The librarian referrer also deals with the director.
Here, unlike the relationship with coworkers, the contributions rule seems again to be most influential. The librarian
performs the job and expects several things in return from
the director. One is to be subjected to only reasonable demands, meaning not being overworked, even if in the director's opinion it is in the interest of providing the user
with the best service possible. Another is to exhibit a
proper balance of interaction in which the director does not
meddle too much in daily procedures but still is available to
assist with a decision when needed. Perhaps in a small library where the director performs public service functions
or in the case of a gregarious director there might be some
of the sociability associated with coworkers, but it did not
seem to be typical.

Another person with whom the librarian may interact
is the outside personal contact. Here the degree of friendship would affect the extent to which the contributions rule
is applied and the type of contributions, economic or social,
expected. In friendly relationships, social contributions
can be used to pay economic debts. The empathy perspective also applies, with both librarians concerned with the

welfare of the other. When dealing with contacts on a less
friendly basis, there is likely to be more of a consciousness
of each library's or each librarian's economic contributions
to the other.

In general, then, the economic aspect of the contributions rule seems to be the main influence on referral relationships with other libraries and is important in dealings
with the director and the user. With the director and the
user, the social aspect of the contributions rule is also important in referral. In addition the impact of the contributions rule in the interaction with the user may be offset
to a degree by idealism, especially the common librarians'
credo of equal service; and by empathy, which is facilitated
by face-to-face encounter.

As regards dealings with coworkers, equality rather
than the contributions rule prevails. Social exchange might
be said to be paramount, although a more emotion-based
perspective, such as empathy, may also be operating. If
sufficiently friendly, relations with outside contacts are
similar to those with coworkers. Otherwise they again involve the economic and social aspects of the contributions
rule.

The prevalence of the economic contributions rule in
dealings between libraries may be theorized to limit referral
since it makes referral a request for assistance that should
receive reimbursement. The operation of the contributions
rule in both its economic and social aspects when assisting
users may again be theorized to limit referral since the user
may be judged to be too low in contributions to merit it.
When instead the librarian disregards contributions from the
user, following the needs rule, referral is encouraged.

The relative lack of concern with measuring contributions in relation to coworkers may be theorized to facilitate
referral since it should lessen hesitation to ask a coworker
for advice. The same is true of sufficiently friendly relations with outside contacts.

The effect on referral of the contributions relationship
between the librarian and the director is less easy to pre-
dict. The librarian may either comply with or seek to sub-
vert what is perceived as unreasonable pressure to either

promote or discourage referral. Directors whose faults are
thought to be not as much in the positions they take as in
a general disinterestedness or unavailability may hinder
referral, or a solution may be found in spite of their lack
of involvement.

Returning to the complex issue of self-interest and
its role in the librarian's motivation, it first ought to be
acknowledged that in guarding against unreimbursed en-
croachments by outsiders, librarians not only protect themselves from overwork but safeguard the resources to be
spent on primary users. Also, the argument is sometimes
made that denial of assistance to outsiders actually may
benefit them by forcing them to take responsibility for
themselves, at least to the extent of buying some basic
level of library service.

Similarly, spending much time with users, especially
students, who seem disinterested would be argued by some
to be "spoiling" them rather than encouraging them to behave responsibily. Devoting more time to help someone
whose position in life appears more socially useful, especially
someone who is in a position to help the library financially,
would be justified by others as serving the long-term interests of all. Thus judgments regarding users' contributions need not be interpreted as self-centered attempts to
evade work, lack of empathy, or lack of idealism. Moreover, the personal satisfactions to be derived from serving
users in an empathic and idealistic manner mean that such
prosocial behavior need not be interpreted as onerous self-
sacrifice.

That dealings with coworkers in referral seemed to be
a positive experience for most librarians perhaps indicates
a generally healthy working environment. The apparent
neglect of nonprofessionals in some libraries could be motivated in most instances by genuine concern that they might
give users inaccurate information. Regarding friendly relations with outside contacts, it was found that depending on
friends rather than regular channels does not always lead
to greater efficiency. Still, on balance it would seem to
open opportunities to the user.

Finally, the reported conflicts with directors, while
self-centered to the extent that some of them related to

being overworked or underappreciated, were also largely
concerned with what librarians considered to be inefficient
practices, such as being forced to pass on trite questions
to backup libraries, that were ultimately costly not only to
these librarians but to their clientele as well.

Overall, then, while the findings indicate more concern with contributions and less with equality or needs in
making assessments about referral, and more motivation by
self-interest and less by empathy or idealism, this is not to
say that in everyone's view librarians have taken the less
conscionable path. As seen, self-interest is allied with others' interest to such an extent that by depriving others we
may benefit not only ourselves but another as well.

Besides equity and empathy, several other personal
qualities were presented in the results chapter. Equity requires that in making a request or a suggestion to another
that tact be employed, and tact was found to be important
in the types of interactions detailed in this study. Three
qualities were related to a feeling of accomplishment:
achievement motivation, independence, and efficiency.
Achievement motivation in the librarian should generally
work to the advantage of the user, although empathy or
idealism may be needed to provide added incentive for librarians when they are doing routine tasks. Examples of
independence centered on rule breaking by librarians.
Some of these may have been instances of the librarian disregarding reasonable restrictions in a headstrong manner,
and others may have been cases in which idealism, or empathy, or assessment of what was due the user made rule
breaking seem necessary. Efficiency in a work situation
was naturally a major consideration, but not an overriding
one. If an act is seen as an efficient means towards an
end, but the end is thought to be inequitable, the act is
unlikely to be performed.

FINAL DEFINITIONS OF LIBRARY REFERRAL

In Chapter 3 library referral was defined in the functional sense of what act the referrer must perform to be said
to have made a referral. At this point a second sentence
will be added to the definition, reflecting more completely
the findings of this study, so that the entire definition now
reads:

An act of library employees of responding to individuals' needs by directing these individuals to
another person, or to a place under the control of
another person, for the fulfillment of these needs.
The act seems to be influenced by the employee's
personal qualities and by various other factors pertaining to the employee's library, the outside resources referred to, and the individual being referred.

As noted in Chapter 3, the referral may be characterized as potentially effective if it is to a person or place
thought to be able to fulfill the need (determining that the
referral was in fact effective would require feedback from
the place referred to or from the individual referred). It
was further noted in Chapter 3 that the referral may be
characterized as potentially efficient for the user if it is to
a person or place both thought to be able to fulfill the need
and approachable without unnecessary loss of the user's
energy, time, money, or materials. Furthermore, the referral may be characterized as potentially efficient for the
library employee or the employee's library if it is done without unnecessary loss of their energy, time, money, or materials. Achieving a balance between what is efficient for the
user and what is efficient for the referring library may be
termed efficient referral policy. Such policy frequently
would include consideration of what is efficient for the person or place referred to, either for practical reasons, such
as fear of being accused of overburdening the outside resource; or for psychological reasons, such as wishing to
avoid a feeling of being in debt; or for ethical considerations
regarding how much should be asked of the outside resource.

One of the purposes of this dissertation was to explore
concepts of "good" referral, and in one sense efficient referral is good referral. However, in view of this study's
discussions of the contributions, equality, and needs rules
of equity; and of the perspectives of self-interest, idealism,
and empathy; plus examination in Appendix A of ethics and
other topics of the initial literature review relating to equity;
it is possible also to suggest that good referral should include some notion of equitable referral.

From the self-interest perspective, equitable referral
would usually be related to the contributions rule, likely

including an evaluation of the user and consideration of
whether the referring institution were taking advantage of
the place being referred to. Those providing service would
expect to be reimbursed in kind or in financial support.

The empathy perspective would emphasize the justification of referral on the basis of equality or need, with the
needy not turned away for lack of contributions. The idealism perspective would be similar to either of the other two
perspectives, depending on the nature of one's ideals, but
would more than likely support the idea of service based on
equality or need than the self-interest point of view, and
would probably be more uniformly applied than is empathy,
which is generally taken to be more emotional and situational.

If differing views can be held as to what constitutes
equitable referral, is there no agreement on what is inequitable referral? In fact there seems to be widespread agreement on one point, that taking advantage of another's generosity but not being generous in return is wrong. At
Kohlberg's Stage 6 moral reasoning such behavior would violate impartiality, and only at Stage 1 would notions of impartiality be completely absent. Accepting aid from another
but not offering aid in return would also violate the empathy
perspective. Even the self-interest perspective would see
danger in taking but not giving, since this would risk punishment by society and also would be contrary to the position
of enlightened self-interest that sees the individual's gain
as inseparable from society's gain. The librarian who feels
justified in telling students from a particular college to return to their own college library for help because they are
not local residents, while at the same time admitting to making perhaps more referrals to that college library than to
any other, would seem to represent moral insensitivity.

IMPLICATIONS FOR FURTHER RESEARCH
AND FOR PRACTICE

The examination of moral reasoning of librarians is an
area requiring further research. An approach similar to
Kohlberg's with a sample of librarians stratified by age,
sex, and other factors, asked to decide the just response
to a set of moral dilemmas, would help to support or disprove
the findings of this study, and would provide new insight
and detail regarding the referral process.

Librarians and library educators might also want to discuss with their coworkers the issues raised here regarding what service is owed to outside users and due from outside institutions. They might consider whether enlightened self-interest, or empathy, or idealism suggests that equity based on equality or needs should be applied more often than what this study found is generally the case-- equity based on contributions.

A number of additional questions for discussion can be posed: What do we think of librarians who deliberately break network protocols to assist their users? Should a seemingly trite question that cannot be answered in-house be turned away gently or should it be referred to another institution? Is enough care taken in referring questions so that the librarian referred to does not have to duplicate the same reference research? Are outsiders given too little assistance, or is more attention sometimes given their questions than to those of the library's primary clientele? Do staff members need to be more courteous to outsiders on the telephone? Should steps be taken to increase personal contacts in other institutions so that referral can be more effective? Do academic librarians need to be better acquainted with faculty members so that the latter do not make unnecessary referrals to other libraries?

Librarians and educators might also benefit from open discussion with their coworkers about the widespread inability to provide adequate travel directions to outside resources in a region, and the variability in librarians' willingness to advise regarding safe travel. If nonprofessionals are to make some referrals, and in many libraries this is likely at least during certain hours, have they been briefed on basic information and procedures? Are written referral aids adequate? Are staff members familiar with the location and obligations of United States documents depositories? What are the advantages of a system of evaluative feedback, and can such a system be achieved economically?

The implications and research issues of this study extend beyond the area of library referral. As was apparent in the chapter on results, some of the factors related to referral are factors that relate to library service in general. Thus, a library employee's act of evaluating how much assistance a user deserves affects other services, not just

referral, and a library where training for referral is inadequate also may provide insufficient training in service attitudes and in the use of in-library materials and techniques.

In addition, research similar to that undertaken in
this study could be directed at many other occupations in
which a service provider finds it necessary to refer some
requests for assistance. One major variation would be fields
in which fees are received from individual clients, causing
practitioners to seek to obtain referrals.

Many of the questions raised in this study pertain to
efficiency, and efficiency along with equity was one of the
two most influential factors found to influence librarians'
decisions relating to referral. Underlying nearly all considerations, however, was equity, the concern over who deserves what.

RELEVANCY OF THE INITIAL LITERATURE REVIEW

INTRODUCTION

Part of the research for this study was an initial literature review, which explored factors suspected of influencing referral. Ultimately this review was divided into ten topics. Relevant portions of each of these topics are discussed below in relation to the results presented in Chapter 3.

TOPICS

Goals

Goals are concerned with the equity issue of who deserves what. At times librarians found themselves at odds with their library administrators over the amount of service that should be provided. Thus, a head of reference countered an administrator's plea that phone bills be reduced with the response that proper service prevents any cutbacks in the use of the telephone in the reference and referral process. Such a situation is predicted by Etzioni (1960, pp. 276-278), who found little interest in non-goal, system functions among professionals, and by Simon (1976), who states that "members of organizations identify with particular subgoals not merely (or mainly) because of the reward structure, but because these subgoals are closest to their daily activities, hence are perceived most clearly" (p. xiv).

Other writers argue that professionals' goals may not
be high minded. Perrow (1961, p. 862) believes that they
may be specialized, narrow, and self-serving; and Osborn,
Hunt, and Jauch (1980, p. 48) state that professional criteria are centered on products and services, not necessarily
systems goals or societal contribution. These suggestions
are reflected in the finding of the indifferent attitude of
some academic library subject specialists towards working
at the general reference desk.

An absence of written policy statements in the libraries
studied makes referral a less clear goal for the organization
than it would be if such statements were in writing. The
excuse offered that a written policy is not needed because
the public does not expect referral and therefore does not
complain if it is lacking suggests that referral may not be
a widely agreed upon goal. Similarly, Robbins (1972) holds
that the reference librarian may be a "street-level bureau-
crat," faced with circumstances in which "expectations about
job performance are ambiguous and/or contradictory and include unattainable idealized dimensions" (p. 1390).

Autonomy in Decision Making

Studies of organizational behavior have shown that
some people enlarge their work beyond its prescribed bound-
aries, some bypass their superiors, and some give other
evidence of an informal system (Argyris, 1968, p. 312).
In accord with this observation, some librarians had an un-
questioning attitude towards the policies and procedures of
their library, outside libraries, and library networks, while
others circumvented what they considered to be unreasonable restrictions. Such circumvention was made easier because their reference work was not closely supervised. Assuming that the autonomy of the reference librarian is at
least as great as that of the classroom teacher, there is
relevancy in Bidwell's (1965, p. 1014) comment that enforc-
ing rules of procedures is likely to be only partially effective, not only because teachers resist authority but also
because teaching is not very observable.

Allied to the issue of employee autonomy is that of
employee participation in decision making. Wilson (1981)
claims that professional education, including that of

librarians, teaches them to expect that they will have some
say over the way in which their work is performed so that
"when a bureaucratic organization such as a library with-
holds such participation, professionals are apt to become
discontented" (p. 288). This contention was borne out at
least as regards those interviewees who complained that
their directors were making unreasonable demands.

Directors in a couple of instances were said not to be
aware of the importance of referral. This may also be true
of some of the directors who refused to participate in the
research project. However, it may be that these directors
were not so much disinterested as uncertain as to what
policies to espouse in an area so filled with difficult equity
issues, especially regarding interaction with other libraries.
Statements in the literature supporting this notion include
those of Osborn et al. (1980, p. 187), who write that since
uncertainty reduces "clout" it can cause managers to with-
draw from leadership, and of Simon (1976, p. 64), who
states that "sometimes the lack of integration in an organization's means-end hierarchy is due to refusal of the policy-
making body to decide a 'hot' issue of policy."

Peer Pressure

The pressure to win acceptance from one's coworkers
may influence how one performs one's duties. In her Rutgers dissertation, Brady (1972, p. 55) found some support
for the hypothesis that a teacher's decision to refer a child
to receive special services would be influenced by the way
he thought the group with whom he identified would behave.
On the other hand, librarians interviewed did not state that
they adapted their reference and referral activities to what
they thought their coworkers would approve of. The autonomy of the interaction with the user and the fact that a
question often can be approached in more than one correct
way perhaps lessened the pressure towards conformity.

However, librarians did seem to be generally in accord
with their libraries' policies and their coworkers' attitudes
and practices pertaining to service to their primary users
and to outsiders. The young librarian who said that service
should be extended liberally to outsiders, while all her more
experienced coworkers said the opposite, seemed remarkably

unacclimatized, as did the relatively new librarian who appeared to be unaware of her coworkers' dissatisfaction with
their backup library. Librarians certainly differed with coworkers in personality and approach, but not so much in
terms of basic orientation.

It was in respect to the question of what service was
due from large private academic ibraries that librarians
seemed most likely to disagree, and this complex issue
evoked mixed reactions from individual librarians also. Belief that information should be shared conflicted with belief
that people have the right to own the sources of information,
and conflicting, strong arguments could be heard from different librarians in the same library and sometimes from the
same librarian.

Training

It is in the specialized area of information and referral
that the library literature is more likely to link referral with
training. An example provided by Childers (1984) is that
of the thorough training at the Library Information Center
(LINC) of the Memphis and Shelby County Public Library:

> The LINC staff are trained vigorously for 6 months,
> during which time they are on probation. For sev-
> eral weeks, they observe back-up operations and
> phone transactions in the LINC center. For several
> weeks after that they listen in on transactions being
> conducted by a trained staff member. Then they
> work one-on-one with another trained staff member,
> answering queries. After that they perform "solo"
> with a trained observer. Then, finally, they work
> on their own. [p. 85]

Such rigorous training did not have a parallel in the
libraries in which interviews were conducted. Indeed, there
did not seem to be as organized an approach to training in
general in the libraries studied as is to be found in Dana's
description in 1912 of the administration of examinations to
library staff, with at least one question related to referral:
"Where in Newark, outside the library, would you send a
person who wishes to see many genealogies?" (pp. 8-9).

One way to help insure effective training is to support it with detailed policy statements. Discussing reference
policy statements in academic libraries, Mary Jo Lynch
(1972) wrote, "Obviously a detailed statement of policy is
useful to new people in a department, but it is also helpful
to experienced staff members who occasionally need to re-
fresh their memories" (pp. 224-225). Librarians interviewed
did not have the benefit of detailed policy statements regarding referral.

Another form of training is to correct people's mistakes
through a feedback procedure. For example, member libraries of the New York Metropolitan Reference and Research
Library Agency (METRO) can offer their users a courtesy
card providing access to other member libraries. Librarians
who receive improper referrals may complain to the library
identified on the card as the referring library. Feedback
procedures are supported by the "Developmental Guidelines"
of the American Library Association's (1979) Reference and
Adult Services Division. These state that referrals "should
be evaluated at selected intervals to determine the effectiveness of the delivery service and the quality of the response
to the user" (p. 276).

Feedback as a training mechanism was not a strong
factor in the libraries in which interviews were conducted.
Networks provided some feedback regarding failures to follow
required procedures. The main feedback from the user was
usually an expression of appreciation to a librarian who had
been especially helpful or perhaps especially pleasant. Such
expressions of appreciation may be viewed in equity terms
as acknowledging a debt of gratitude or repaying kindness
with kindness.

Personality

Schmidt (1975, pp. 36-37) reviewed nine studies of
librarians' personalities and deduced a typical personality
profile marked by a lack of aggressiveness, a passive attitude towards authority, and a well developed sense of order.
Interview data was insufficient to judge regarding aggressiveness and sense of order. A passive attitude towards
authority was not obvious among those interviewed. Criticism was directed against authority when it was thought to

have been wielded unfairly or inefficiently, and some librarians told of disobeying their superiors' orders or network rules.

Clayton (1970, p. 397) reports that evidence indicates that librarians tend to be refugees from professions that are strongly competitive, such as the arts and literature, or that have considerable stress, such as teaching. The library school students studied by Clayton were also patient, sympathetic, and appreciative.

As to whether librarians are refugees from stressful occupations, descriptions of busy periods at the reference desk were calm accounts of hectic situations. While not happy when users could not be given sufficient attention, interviewees sounded as though they coped at least with this amount of stress.

The suggestion that librarians exhibit patience and sympathy received some support. The Exemplary Referrer's description of interest and satisfaction gained in drawing out a shy student seems to be at the very essence of the profession. This is not to deny that librarians confessed to moments of laziness or indifference, or that librarians who are generally unhelpful went unmentioned.

Embarrassment

Brock (1977, p. 1134) speculated that his finding that less experienced physicians refer less is because they are less confident and hesitate to have their professional peers see patients that they have been managing. In literature pertaining to libraries, Hutchins wrote in 1944 (p. 36) that ignorance and pride can prevent a question from being referred from one department to another in a library.

The librarian would seem to be vulnerable to embarrassment and wounded pride when exposing his or her ignorance to a user, an immediate coworker, someone in another department, or someone in an outside organization to which a referral is made. The possibility of embarrassment stemming from referral may, of course, vary with the likelihood that the librarian receiving the referral will learn who made it. For the librarian who lacks confidence, a

referral actually may be less embarrassing than turning to
a coworker and asking if some in-house source has been
overlooked.

Overall, librarians interviewed did not admit to as
much concern over embarrassment during referral as might
have been expected. One person reported that a librarian
at a backup library had told her once that the information
she was seeking could have been found in her own library,
but this advice was said to have been offered tactfully,
and she did not seem to have found it embarrassing. Directing users to places to which they are not allowed entry
can cause embarrassment, and a couple of librarians admitted to having done so, but these were said to have been
rare instances and not recent. There was some indication
that a newly hired reference librarian may feel self-conscious
about asking many questions and may spend more time working on problems than is necessary, yet the new person
seems likely to outgrow this. Finally, a few interviewees
said that they felt some embarrassment over shortcomings
in their collections, which would seem to be less embarrassing than a personal failing.

Ethics

"Ethics" can mean both the standards of morality that
apply to people in respect generally to their living among
other people, and the standards by which a particular group
or community decides to regulate its behavior (Dictionary of
Philosophy, 1984, p. 112). The latter includes professional
ethics, which is the principal concern here.

Service to the point of self-sacrifice is prominent
among librarians, claim Naegele and Stolar (1960, p. 2891).
While acknowledging that a librarian may be concerned about
an audit by a governing body, Kaser (1974) observes that a
librarian who does not give the highest priority to equality
of access to information is frequently thought to manifest
"the Natural Depravity of Man" (p. 280). Trezza (1972),
at the time he was serving as director of the Illinois State
Library, wrote: "True cooperation is unselfish cooperation.
It is never equal" (p. 319). Regarding this emphasis on
equality of access, Blasingame (1979, p. 1821) points out
that present library programs and standards are guided by

Carleton Joeckel's evangelistic call in 1935 for library service for all residents of the country.

A fundamental question is whether librarians really are
motivated by generosity, or whether apparent generosity is
granted with the expectation of receiving kindness in return. An example of the latter is Hamlin's (1964) caution:

> Every college and university librarian must recognize
> that the students for whom he is responsible are
> going to be seeking admittance into hundreds of
> other libraries, public and institutional, across the
> country. If he cares about the treatment his stu-
> dents will receive, he should also give a thought to
> the visitors at his own door. [p. 66]

Walster, Walster and Berscheid (1978, p. 101) note that
most social scientists take a cynical view of altruism. They
themselves present an "Equity Theory," which assumes that
people perform acts that are rewarded, but that if they take
more than they deserve they feel distress due to either a
fear of retaliation or a loss of self-esteem (p. 22).

An analysis of resolutions and recommendations preliminary to the 1979 White House Conference on Library and
Information Services (King Research, Inc., 1979) shows consideration for both the needs of users and the burdens
placed on those libraries that are called upon to share their
resources. Resolutions included the notion that "communities
should adopt policies of resource sharing which would eliminate barriers to direct patron access through reciprocal borrowing, interlibrary loan passes, and reference lists of library materials, both print and nonprint, or collections not
permitted to be circulated" (p. 77), and that "the State
library should investigate the possibility of implementing a
statewide library card system...." (p. 78). On the other
hand, concern for overburdened libraries is found in resolutions that "a study should be undertaken to examine the
problems encountered by private, academic and special libraries in permitting public access to their facilities" (p.
77), and that "State funding is required to develop multitype library cooperative districts needed to promote a com-
prehensive approach to information and research problems"
(p. 78).

The American Library Association also has shown concern for both access to information and for the rights of
individual institutions. Access to information was adopted
as the primary priority at the association's 1981 annual conference (Breivik, 1981, p. 615), while in 1979 the association's Reference and Adult Services Division adopted a
statement on "Ethics of Service," advising that "eligibility
of users will be determined by the role, scope, and mission
of individual institutions" (p. 277).

The issue of generosity versus self-interest is not
always clear-cut. The director of a public university's law
library argued against easy access for students from a
smaller law library into a large one because the host library
renders "a disservice to the other institution by making it
possible for it to remain deficient" (Allen, 1973, p. 169).
Apparently the suggestion here is that funds would be found
to bolster the small library's collection if there were not a
large library it could depend on.

At other times selfishness is obvious, as in the case
of some depositories for U.S. Government publications. Although these depository libraries are obligated by law to
make the publications accessible to the general public, in
August 1979 the Government Printing Office found it necessary to send depositories a preprint of an article reporting
that a number of them "appear to be hindering public access to government collections" (Armstrong and Russell,
1979).

Unequal service does not only relate to discriminating
between primary clientele and outsiders. Halmos (1970, p.
30) warns that professionals must try to resist the tempta-
tion to discriminate between clients on grounds that are not
relevant to the discharge of professional duty. In a literature review of altruism, Krebs (1970) reported that "although few studies purposefully manipulated the variable,
it seems likely that interpersonal attractiveness incidentally
influenced the responses of benefactors in many studies"
(pp. 297-298). The ethical librarian would be expected to
guard against allowing factors such as attractiveness to
determine the level of service. Bekker (1977, p. 224) in
his dissertation on the ethics of librarianship agrees with
McGlothlin (1960, p. 214) that priorities should be in the
descending order of society and state, clients, profession
and colleagues, agency, and self-interest.

Whether librarians do place society's interest before
their own is disputed. Denzin and Mettlin (1968, p. 381)
think that neither pharmacy nor librarianship has been able
to recruit adequately committed persons and to develop hu-
manitarian values. Robinson (1978, p. 24) charges that
professionals' claims to expertise, objectivity, autonomy,
and a service ethic are no longer accepted at face value
by sociologists. Rules of professionals are aligned with their
own interest, and clients are largely powerless, he says
(p. 36).

Reeves (1980, p. 104) makes note of the argument
that librarians are not professionals because they lack
autonomy in organizational work settings. A librarian's
desire to do what is ethical may be blocked by the policies
of the employing organization. Social scientists have pointed
out, however, that some employees exhibit considerable independence. Reissman's (1949, p. 309) "functional bureau-
crat" feels no conflict between his professional ethic and
his job because only the former standard exists for him.
"Cosmopolitans," as described by Gouldner (1957, p. 293),
are low in organizational loyalty, high in commitment to
specialized skills, and high in orientation to outside reference groups.

Of all the topics of the initial literature review, that
of ethics is most relevant to the major findings of this study
concerning equity, and for this reason it has been presented
here with little reduction in content compared to some of the
other topics.

The discussion began with idealistic statements about
librarians' self-sacrifice and dedication to the principle of
equality of access to information. There followed a contrast-
ing perspective of acting out of self-interest, so that even
apparent altruism is performed with the expectation of some
repayment.

The results of this study tend to support the second
view. Service to outsiders seemed to be motivated more by
the thought of receiving some benefit in return, such as
reciprocal service or a good public image. Librarians were
generally accepting of their institutions' restrictions on
service to outsiders, with only occasional rule bending hint-
ing at an autonomous personal position being taken. If the

call for equal access is taken as the professional standard,
librarians interviewed did not for the most part make statements that would label themselves "cosmopolitans," low in
organizational loyalty and high in orientation to outside reference groups, who would uphold such a professional
standard at the cost of peace in the workplace.

A major ethical requirement is consideration of the
welfare of one's users, ranked by McGlothlin only after
obligations to society and state. It is not always easy to
judge what is society's due and what is due the immediate
user. In weighing the equity of restrictions imposed on
their users by outside institutions, interviewees gave a
range of responses, including objecting to the restrictions,
objecting but at the same time being somewhat sympathetic,
and being completely accepting. Objections referred at
times to an imbalance in exchange: The restrictive library
was felt to receive benefits but not to extend benefits. At
other times the argument was based on need: Some users
with a need for information could not afford user fees or
otherwise overcome the restrictive barriers.

Service to users such as those whom interviewees described as being overdemanding, disinterested, or unpleasant presented another ethical challenge. The professional's
service ethic would ordinarily require a generous spirit.
On the other hand, time spent with a difficult user is often
time denied another task, and perhaps users need to be
made aware that they must not make unreasonable demands.

Institutional Cooperation

Despite what appear to be unassailable arguments for
cooperation among organizations, such efforts frequently
have little success (Hawley, 1977). In a study of higher
education consortia, Forbis (1973) discovered that when
librarians demonstrated success at cooperation, local facul-
ties considered it a threat to autonomy and became even
more protective of their prerogatives. Dyer (1978) terms
her study of Cooperation in Library Service to Children "a
refresher course in institutional rigidity" (p. 94). She
writes that staffs in both public and school libraries "are
reluctant to cooperate with their counterparts; seeing col-
laborative ventures as threats to autonomy and as territorial

infringements, staff members jealously guard their respective bailiwicks and rebuff entreaties to cooperate" (92).

The most specific response relating to fear of loss of autonomy through cooperation in the present study was that of the reference head who said that cooperative collection building with a nearby library had to be kept informal so that funding authorities could not argue that it was a reason for reduced financial support. In some libraries there also appeared to be a hesitancy to refer to or to telephone other libraries, perhaps due to a concern for autonomy.

Interdependence among organizations can also mean that some are overloaded with outside requests for assistance. Cumming (1968) mentions that the clergyman felt role strain when performing referrals since "other agencies were not always happy about either accepting his clients or cooperating with him in their care" (p. 97). Librarians interviewed did not often receive an unpleasant response from another library, but the fear of making unwarrantable demands did create a degree of stress.

Investigating the referral of antisocial children to a community agency, Feldman, Goodman, and Wodarski (1976, p. 272) found that some referral problems were caused by agencies referring inappropriate clients when their staff was excessively overburdened. Among librarians interviewed, making inappropriate referrals when overburdened was claimed to be a rare occurrence. Another cause of unnecessary referrals, in a hospital's program to train nurses to make referrals to community nursing agencies, was thought to be over-enthusiasm (Moreland and Schmitt, 1974, p. 97). Librarians said that over-enthusiasm was characteristic of some referrals made by campus faculty to outside libraries.

Outside Personal Contacts

Clements and Kyle (1975, p. 24) believe that personal acquaintanceship with as many individual librarians as possible is a necessary adjunct to community information and referral services, and Childers (1981) criticized a library reference text because it "never deals adequately with the formal and informal networks that link the local library with

other libraries and nonlibrary sources of information." This
study also found that personal contacts outside of one's
workplace are of assistance in making referrals.

Building a network of personal contacts is usually
a gradual process based on the librarian's work and personal experiences in a particular geographic area. A number of contacts can be made in one day, however. For example, Corazzini and Shelton (1974) propose a yearly "referral bazaar," which would "introduce campus professionals
to the names and phone numbers, and specialization of various persons in receiving agencies" (p. 463). Among the
libraries studied there was no example of such an event,
but there were reports of informal and formal visits, meetings, and conferences at which librarians made useful contacts. In addition, some librarians told of forming friendly
relationships by telephone, without even making face-to-face
encounters.

Cost to the Client

"Cost" as used here includes both psychological and
physical dimensions (travel time to a library being a physical
cost). Gerstberger and Allen (1968) concluded that

> engineers, in selecting among information channels,
> act in a manner which is intended not to maximize
> gain, but rather to minimize loss. The loss to be
> minimized is the cost of effort, either physical or
> psychological, which must be expended in order to
> gain access to an information channel. [p. 277]

D'Elia (1980, pp. 425-426) found that users of the public
library tended to perceive it as more accessible than did
non-users. In addition, an Association of Research Libraries
report (1981) states that "students at neighboring high
schools, colleges, and universities, and scholars at nearby
institutions are more apt to consult their own convenience
and the accessibility of materials than to consider academic
affiliation as the prime determinant of library use" (p. 1).

At times cost considerations may involve weighing the
benefits to the user of in-person access versus interlibrary
loan. In-person access may provide quicker access to needed

material, plus access to reference material that can not be
borrowed. It also permits browsing, said by Fussler and
Simon (1977, p. 112) to account for fifty-six percent of a
sample of physics and history volumes removed from the
shelves by users in a large university library, and reported
by Weech (1978, p. 182) to account for much of the faculty
access to separate document collections in academic libraries.
On the other hand, interlibrary loan saves the user travel
time, and browsing can be viewed as a time-consuming alternative to the knowledgeable use of bibliographic and
other reference tools.

One of the most common findings in this study was
that librarians referred with convenience of location in mind,
and that this was reported as also a prime concern of most
users. Interlibrary loan was heavily promoted in a couple
of small public libraries, but the time required to process
interlibrary loan requests discouraged its use in some other
libraries. Librarians did not seem to be suggesting in-
person use rather than interlibrary loan because of the advantages of browsing provided by in-person access.

Not predicted in the literature reviewed was the frequent lack of preparedness to provide users with specific
travel directions. Nor was the influence that fear of travel
to inner cities has on librarians' referral practices forseen.

CONCLUSION

Many of the ideas in the initial literature review were
supported by the results of this study, and the central theme
of equity helps to give unity and greater significance to the
results.

The first topic of the review, "Goals," is largely concerned with the equity issue of who deserves what. At
times librarians found themselves at odds with their library
administration over the amount of service that should be
provided. Similarly, the topic of "Autonomy in Decision
Making" pertains to equity in that some reference librarians
feel that they are owed the freedom to select the best way
to accomplish certain goals, such as incurring long distance
telephone charges to assist users. In terms of their "Personality," another topic, librarians were not so passive

towards authority as not to express independent opinions and reveal independent actions regarding equity issues of how much service to provide.

Concerning the topic of "Peer Pressure," a desire to conform may have been present in the relative lack of conflict within each library over the degree of service that should be offered to primary clientele and to outsiders. However, pertaining to the topic of "Ethics," two issues that did cause differences of opinion among peers were that of how much service should be offered to overdemanding, disinterested, or unpleasant users; and that of how justified are the restrictions imposed on outsiders by other institutions.

As for the topic of "Institutional Cooperation," some academic librarians complained about faculty who were too eager to burden other institutions with students who should have been directed instead to their own campus library. Relating to both "Institutional Cooperation" and "Ethics," librarians most often sought equity relationships in which their library was neither overly dependent nor overly generous. "Outside Personal Contacts," another topic, connects with equity in that through the bonds of friendship librarians may be said to both owe and be owed assistance.

Several topics relate equity to errors by librarians. Organized feedback, discussed under the topic of "Training," may be scarce in part because of a feeling among librarians that they are owed protection from "Embarrassment," also a topic. In other aspects of their jobs, being corrected in a tactful manner seems to save librarians from embarrassment.

That training regarding referral is often inadequate may indicate a lack of conviction that referral is an important service that is due users. The same may be said of travel directions, which pertain to the topic of "Cost to the Client" and which can save the user time but do not seem to be viewed as important by many librarians. Another possibility is that librarians do not give more attention to referral training and to travel directions because they fear creating the appearance of being too eager to take advantage of the places to which they make referrals.

APPENDIX B

LETTER TO LIBRARY DIRECTORS

[TYPED ON LETTERHEAD OF PH.D. PROGRAM
IN LIBRARY AND INFORMATION STUDIES]

[Date]

[Name and address of library director]

Dear [Name of director],

As part of my doctoral work in library studies at Rutgers University, I will be studying and characterizing the referral process in a variety of libraries. To accomplish this I must interview reference librarians. Your library is one of those in which I would like to conduct interviews on a single day sometime in the next few months with at least two, and ideally three or four, librarians. Each interview will last about an hour and will be tape recorded. The tapes will be listened to only by me, and the identities of the libraries and the librarians will not be disclosed. This will be a general study about referral, not an evaluation of individuals or libraries. I would hope to start early in the morning, and any clarification needed following the day of the interviews would most likely be done through brief phone calls.

163

Enclosed is a postcard for you to indicate whether or not your library will participate. It includes spaces for the name and phone number of the person I should contact to set a date and time for the visit and who could assist me in setting up the interviews. The pace at which I call these contact people will be governed in part by the extent to which each day's interviewing presents new ideas to be evaluated and developed into new lines of questioning as I visit the several participating libraries.

Besides interviewing, I would spend some time familiarizing myself with your library and its setting, since I am looking for whatever may influence the act of referral. Any relevant information you or your staff could furnish during the visit, such as specialized network membership, preexisting written reference and referral policy, and number of recorded referrals, would be appreciated.

Although I realize how difficult it can be to arrange busy work schedules to allow time for research projects, I hope you will be able to participate in what should be an interesting study. I will gladly send a summary of my findings about referral to you at the completion of the project.

Sincerely,

[Signed]
George Hawley

REPLY POSTCARD

[Library   [(will)
(will not) participate in the study of
the referral process.

(if yes) Name and phone number of
person to be contacted:

_____

_____

date _____

signed _____

REFERENCES

Allen, Cameron (1973). Whom we shall serve: Secondary patrons of the university law school library. Law Library Journal, 66, 161-171.

American Library Association, Reference and Adult Services Division (1979). A commitment to information services: Developmental guidelines. RQ, 18, 275-278.

Argyris, Chris (1968). Organizations: Effectiveness. In David L. Sills (Ed.), International encyclopedia of the social sciences (Vol. 11, pp. 311-319). New York: Macmillan.

Armstrong, Anne, & Russell, Judith C. (1979). Public access?: Not always, a survey of depository libraries reveals. Information World, 1(9), 1, 11.

Association of Research Libraries, Systems and Procedures Exchange Center (1981). External user services (Spec Flyer No. 73). Washington, DC: Association of Research Libraries.

Bar-Tal, Daniel (1976). Prosocial behavior: Theory and research. Washington, DC: Hemisphere.

Batson, C. Daniel, & Coke, Jay S. (1981). Empathy: A source of altruistic motivation for helping? In J. Philippe Rushton & Richard M. Sorrentino (Eds.), Altruism and helping behavior: Social, personality, and developmental perspectives (pp. 167-187). Hillside, NJ: Lawrence Erlbaum.

Bekker, Johan (1977). Professional ethics and its application to librarianship (Doctoral dissertation, Case Western Reserve University, 1976). Dissertation Abstracts International, 38, 10A.

Bidwell, Charles E. (1965). The school as a formal organization. In James G. March (Ed.), Handbook of Organizations (pp. 972-1022). Chicago: Rand McNally.

Blasingame, Ralph (1979). The public library and information policy. Library Journal, 104, 1818-1822.

Blau, Peter M. (1964). Exchange and power in social life. New York: John Wiley.

Blau, Peter M. (1968). Interaction: Social exchange. In David L. Sills (Ed.), International encyclopedia of the social sciences (Vol. 7, pp. 452-458). New York: Macmillan.

Brady, Patricia M. (1972). Decision theory analysis of referrals by teachers to school special services (Doctoral dissertation, Rutgers University). Dissertation Abstracts International, 33, 1505A.

Breivik, Patricia S. (1981). Implementing the new priorities. Library Journal, 106, 615, 618.

Brock, Carol (1977). Consultation and referral patterns of family physicians. The Journal of Family Practice, 4, 1129-1134.

Brown, George W. (1973). Some thoughts on grounded theory. Sociology, 7, 1-16.

Burchfield, R. W. (Ed.) (1982). A supplement to the Oxford English dictionary (Vol. 3). New York: Oxford.

Childers, Thomas (1979). Trends in public library I&R services. Library Journal, 104, 2035-2039.

Childers, Thomas (1980). The test of reference. Library Journal, 105, 924-928.

Childers, Thomas (1981). [Review of The librarian and reference queries]. Journal of Academic Librarianship, 7, 239.

Childers, Thomas (1983). Information and referral: Public libraries. Norwood, NJ: Ablex.

Clayton, Howard (1970). Femininity and job satisfaction among male library students at one Midwestern university. College & Research Libraries, 31, 388-398.

Clements, C. Justin, & Kyle, Sandra L. (1975). Can anybody out there help me?, RQ, 15, 19-24.

Cook, Karen S., & Messick, David M. (1983). Psychological and sociological perspectives on distributive justice: Convergent, divergent, and parallel lines. In D. M. Messick & K. S. Cook (Eds.), Equity theory: Psychological and sociological perspectives (pp. 1-12). New York: Praeger.

Corazzini, John G., & Shelton, John (1974). A conceptualization of the referral process. Journal of College Student Personnel, 15, 461-464.

Cronbach, Lee J. (1975). Beyond the two disciplines of scientific psychology. American Psychologist, 30, 116-127.

Cuber, John F., & Harroff, Peggy B. (1965). The significant Americans: A study of sexual behaviour among the affluent. New York: Appleton-Century.

Cumming, Elaine (1968). Systems of social regulation. New York: Atherton.

Dana, John C. (1912). Staff examinations. Public Libraries, 17, 8-9.

Darley, John M., & Latané, Bibb (1970). Norms and normative behavior: Field studies of social interdependence. In J. Macaulay & L. Berkowitz (Eds.), Altruism and

helping behavior: Social psychological studies of some
antecedents and consequences (pp. 83-101). New York:
Academic.

D'Elia, George (1980). The development and testing of a
conceptual model of public library user behavior. Library Quarterly, 50, 410-430.

Denzin, Norman K., & Mettlin, Curtis J. (1968). Incom-
plete professionalization: The case of pharmacy. Social
Forces, 46: 375-381.

Deutsch, Morton (1982). Interdependence and psychological
orientation. In Valerian J. Derlega & Janusz Grzelak
(Eds.), Cooperation and helping behavior: Theories and
research (pp. 15-42). New York: Academic.

Deutscher, Irwin (1970). Words and deeds: Social science
and social policy. In William J. Filstead (Ed.), Qualitative
methodology: Firsthand involvement with the social world
(pp. 27-51). Chicago: Markham.

Dickinson, Karen R.; Novick, Lloyd F.; & Asnes, Russell S.
(1976). A study of child health station referrals to
treatment facilities to determine continuity in health
services. Public Health Reports, 91, 138-140.

A dictionary of philosophy (2nd ed.) (1984). New York:
St. Martin's.

Directory of special libraries and information centers (8th
ed.) (1983). Detroit: Gale Research.

Dyer, Esther R. (1978). Cooperation in library service to
children. Metuchen, NJ: Scarecrow.

Eisenberg, Nancy, & Lennon, Randy (1983). Sex differences
in empathy and related capacities. Psychological Bulletin,
94, 100-131.

Elkins, Daniel E. (1983). Factors influencing psychological
referral practices of ministers of the Tennessee Annual
Conference of the United Methodist Church (Doctoral dissertation, George Peabody College of Teachers of Vander-
bilt University). Dissertation Abstracts International,
44, 1234B.

Encyclopedia of associations (19th ed.) (1985). Detroit:
    Gale Research.

Etzioni, Amitai (1960). Two approaches to organizational
    analysis: A critique and a suggestion. Administrative
    Science Quarterly, 5, 257-278.

Feldman, Ronald A.; Goodman, Mortimer; & Wodarski, John
    S. (1976). Inter-agency referrals and the establishment
    of a community-based treatment program. Journal of
    Community Psychology, 4, 269-274.

Feshbach, Norma D. (1982). Sex differences in empathy
    and social behavior in children. In Nancy Eisenberg
    (Ed.), The development of prosocial behavior (pp. 315-
    359). New York: Academic.

Fisher, Jeffrey D.; DePaulo, Bella M.; & Nadler, Arie
    (1981). Extending altruism beyond the altruistic act:
    The mixed effects of and on the help recipient. In J.
    Philippe Rushton & Richard M. Sorrentino (Eds.), Altru-
    ism and helping behavior: Social, personality, and de-
    velopmental perspectives (pp. 367-422). Hillsdale, NJ:
    Lawrence Erlbaum.

Fisher, Jeffrey D., & Nadler, Arie (1982). Determinants of
    recipient reactions to aid: Donor-recipient similarity and
    preconceived dimensions of problems. In Thomas A. Wills
    (Ed.), Basic processes in helping relationships (pp. 131-
    153). New York: Academic.

Forbis, Yates M. (1973). The role of college libraries in
    the planning, development, and operation of educational
    programs in multi-purpose higher education corsortia.
    Washington, DC: Council on Library Resources. (ERIC
    Document Reproduction Service no. ED 079 981).

Fussler, Herman H., & Simon, Julian L. (1961). Patterns
    in the use of books in large research libraries. Chicago:
    University of Chicago Library. Cited by Robert J.
    Greene (1977), The effectiveness of browsing, College
    & Research Libraries, 38, 313.

Gellner, E. A. (1964). Model (theoretical model). In Julius
    Gould & William L. Kolb (Eds.), A dictionary of the social
    sciences (p. 435). New York: Free Press.

Gerstberger, Peter G., & Allen, Thomas J. (1968). Criteria used by research and development engineers in the selection of an information source. Journal of Applied Psychology, 52, 272-279.

Gilligan, Carol (1982). In a different voice: Psychological theory and women's development. Cambridge: Harvard.

Glaser, Barney G. (1978). Theoretical sensitivity: Advances in the methodology of grounded theory. Mill Valley, CA: Sociology Press.

Glaser, Barney G., & Strauss, Anselm L. (1965). Awareness of dying. Chicago: Aldine.

Glaser, Barney G., & Strauss, Anselm L. (1967). The discovery of grounded theory: Strategies for qualitative research. New York: Aldine.

Gouldner, Alvin W. (1957). Cosmopolitans and locals: Toward an analysis of latent social roles--I. Administrative Science Quarterly, 2, 281-306.

Halmos, Paul (1970). The personal service society. New York: Schocken.

Hamlin, Arthur T. (1964). Commentary [on "Assessing the Availability of Resources"]. In American Library Association, Student use of libraries (pp. 62-66). Chicago: American Library Association.

Hawley, George S. (1977). The failure of college-level library cooperation in Newark: An administrative analysis. Unpublished master's thesis. Baruch College of the City University of New York.

Hoffman, Martin L. (1981). The development of empathy. In J. Philippe Rushton & Richard M. Sorrentino (Eds.), Altruism and helping behavior: Social, personality, and developmental perspectives (pp. 41-63). Hillsdale, NJ: Lawrence Erlbaum.

Hoffman, Martin L. (1982). Development of prosocial motivation: Empathy and guilt. In Nancy Eisenberg (Ed.), The development of prosocial behavior (pp. 281-313). New York: Academic.

Hollander, Edwin P. (1980). Leadership and social exchange processes. In Kenneth J. Gergen, Martin S. Greenberg, & Richard H. Willis (Eds.), Social exchange: Advances in theory and research (pp. 103-118). New York: Plenum.

Homans, George C. (1961). Social behavior: Its elementary forms. New York: Harcourt, Brace & World.

Homans, George C. (1982). Foreward. In Jerald Greenberg & Ronald L. Cohen (Eds.), Equity and justice in social behavior (pp. xi-xviii). New York: Academic.

Hong, Barry A., & Wiehe, Vernon R. (1974). Referral patterns of clergy. Journal of Psychology and Theology, 2, 291-297.

Hutchins, Margaret (1944). Introduction to reference work. Chicago: American Library Association.

Joeckel, Carleton B. (1935). The government of the American public library. Chicago: University of Chicago.

Johnson, Knowlton W. (1972). Police interaction and referral activity with personnel of other social regulatory agencies: A multivariate analysis (Doctoral dissertation, Michigan State University, 1971). Dissertation Abstracts International, 32, 6564A.

Kaplan, Abraham (1964). The conduct of inquiry: Methodology for behavioral science. New York: Chandler.

Kaser, David (1974). Library access and the mobility of users. College & Research Libraries, 35, 280-284.

King Research, Inc. (1979). Issues and resolutions: A summary of pre-conference activities (At head of title: White House Conference on Library and Information Services). Washington, DC: National Commission on Libraries and Information Science.

Kohlberg, Lawrence (1981). Essays on moral development: Vol. 1.: The philosophy of moral development: Moral stages and the idea of justice. San Francisco: Harper & Row.

Kohlberg, Lawrence (1984). Essays on moral development:

Vol. 2: The psychology of moral development: The
nature and validity of moral stages. San Francisco:
Harper & Row.

Krebs, Dennis (1970). Altruism--an examination of the
concept and a review of the literature. Psychological
Bulletin, 73, 258-302.

Krebs, Dennis (1978). A cognitive-developmental approach
to altruism. In Lauren Wispé (Ed.), Altruism, sympathy,
and helping: Psychological and sociological principles
(pp. 141-164). New York: Academic.

Krebs, Dennis (1982). Prosocial behavior, equity, and jus-
tice. In Jerald Greenberg & Ronald L. Cohen (Eds.),
Equity and justice in social behavior (pp. 261-308).
New York: Academic.

Lee, Ronald R. (1976). Referral as an act of pastoral care.
The Journal of Pastoral Care, 30, 186-197.

Lerner, Melvin J., & Meindl, James R. (1981). Justice and
altruism. In J. Philippe Rushton & Richard M. Sorrentino (Eds.), Altruism and helping behavior: Social, personality, and developmental perspectives (pp. 213-232).
Hillsdale, NJ: Lawrence Erlbaum.

Leventhal, Gerald S. (1980). What should be done with
equity theory?: New approaches to the study of fairness
in social relationships. In Kenneth J. Gergen, Martin S.
Greenberg, & Richard H. Willis, Social exchange: Advances in theory and research (pp. 27-55). New York:
Plenum.

Levine, Sol, & White, Paul E. (1961). Exchange as a conceptual framework for the study of interorganizational
relationships. Administrative Science Quarterly, 5, 583-
601.

Lynch, Mary Jo (1972). Academic library reference policy
statements. RQ, 11, 222-226.

MacIntyre, Alasdair (1984). After virtue: A study in moral
theory (2nd ed.). Notre Dame, IN: University of Notre
Dame.

Major, Brenda, & Deaux, Kay (1982). Individual differences
    in justice behavior. In Jerald Greenberg & Ronald L.
    Cohen, Equity and justice in social behavior (pp. 43-76).
    New York: Academic.

McClintock, Charles G., & Keil, Linda J. (1982). Equity
    and social exchange. In Jerald Greenberg & Ronald L.
    Cohen (Eds.), Equity and justice in social behavior (pp.
    337-387). New York: Academic.

McClure, Charles R., & Hernon, Peter (1983). Improving
    the quality of reference service for government publica-
    tions. Chicago: American Library Association.

McGlothlin, William J. (1960). Patterns of professional edu-
    cation. New York: Putnam. Cited by Johan Bekker,
    Professional ethics and its application to librarianship,
    p. 224 (Doctoral dissertation, Case Western Reserve
    University, 1976). Dissertation Abstracts International,
    38, 10A.

Messick, David M., & Sentis, Keith (1983). Fairness, pref-
    erence, and fairness biases. In David M. Messick &
    Karen S. Cook (Eds.), Equity theory: Psychological and
    sociological perspectives (pp. 61-94). New York:
    Praeger.

Metcalfe, David H., & Sischy, David (1974). Patterns of
    referral from family practice. The Journal of Family
    Practice, 1, 34-38.

Mischel, Walter, & Mischel, Harriet N. (1976). A cognitive
    social-learning approach to morality and self-regulation.
    In Thomas Lickona (Ed.), Moral development and behavior:
    Theory, research, and social issues (pp. 84-107). New
    York: Holt, Rinehart and Winston.

Mo, Linn (1978). An adventure in exploratory research.
    Acta Sociologica, 21, 165-177.

Moreland, Helen J., & Schmitt, Virginia C. (1974). Making
    referrals is everybody's business. American Journal of
    Nursing, 74, 96-97.

Murray, Sir James A. H. (Ed.) (1910). A new dictionary

on historical principles. Oxford, England: Clarendon,
Vol. 8, part 1: Q nd r, by W. A. Craigie.

Naegele, Kaspar D., & Stolar, Elaine C. (1960). Income
and prestige. Library Journal, 85, 2888-2891.

Noddings, Nel (1984). Caring: A feminine approach to
ethics & moral education. Berkeley: University of
California.

Nolting, Orrin F. (1969). Mobilizing total resources for effective service. Chicago: American Library Association.
Cited by Betty J. Turock, Performance, organization and
attitude: Factors in multitype library networking, pp.
31-33 (Doctoral dissertation, Rutgers University, 1981).
Dissertation Abstracts International, 43, 963A.

Nord, Walter R. (1980). The study of organizations through
a resource-exchange paradigm. In Kenneth J. Gergen,
Martin S. Greenberg, & Richard H. Willis (Eds.), Social
exchange: Advances in theory and research (pp. 119-
139). New York: Plenum.

Osborn, Richard N.; Hunt, James G.; & Jauch, Lawrence
R. (1980). Organization theory: An integrated approach.
New York: John Wiley.

Paritzky, Richard S. (1981). Training peer counselors:
The art of referral. Journal of College Student Personnel, 22, 528-532.

Perrow, Charles (1961). The analysis of goals in complex
organizations. American Sociological Review, 26, 854-866.

Rabbie, Jacob M. (1982). The effects of intergroup competition and cooperation on intragroup and intergroup
relationships. In Valerian J. Derlega & Janusz Grzelak
(Eds.), Cooperation and helping behavior: Theories and
research (pp. 123-149). New York: Academic.

The Random House dictionary of the English language (Unabridged ed.) (1966). New York: Random House.

Reeves, William J. (1980). Librarians as professionals: The
occupation's impact on library work arrangements. Lexington, MA: Lexington Books.

Reissman, Leonard (1949). A study of role conceptions in
    bureaucracy. Social Forces, 3, 305-310.

Robbins, Jane (1972). The reference librarian: A street-
    level bureaucrat? Library Journal, 97, 1389-1392.

Robinson, Tim (1978). In worlds apart: Professionals and
    their clients in the welfare state. London: Bedford
    Square Press of the National Council of Social Service.

Rosenhan, D. L. (1978). Toward resolving the altruism
    paradox: Affect, self-reinforcement, and cognition. In
    Lauren Wispé (Ed.), Altruism, sympathy, and helping:
    Psychological and sociological principles (pp. 101-113).
    New York: Academic.

Rushton, J. Philippe (1981). The altruistic personality.
    In J. Philippe Rushton & Richard M. Sorrentino (Eds.),
    Altruism and helping behavior: Social, personality, and
    developmental perspectives (pp. 251-266). Hillsdale, NJ:
    Lawrence Erlbaum.

Schmidt, C. James (1975). Librarians with the doctorate:
    A survey of selected attitudes and opinions (Doctoral
    dissertation, Florida State University). Dissertation
    Abstracts International, 36, 587A.

Scott, Eric J.; Dean, Debra; Johnston, Julia; & Nussbaum,
    Lenell (1979). Case disposition: An assessment of lit-
    erature on police referral practices. Wshington, DC:
    National Institute of Law Enforcement and Criminal Jus-
    tice.

Simon, Herbert A. (1976). Administrative behavior (3rd
    ed.). New York: Free Press.

Spence, Janet T., & Helmreich, Robert L. (1983). Achieve-
    ment-related motives and behaviors. In Janet T. Spence
    (Ed.), Achievement and achievement motives: Psycho-
    logical and sociological approaches (pp. 7-74). San
    Francisco, CA: W. H. Freeman.

Staub, Ervin (1978). Positive social behavior and morality:
    Vol. 1. Social and personal influences. New York:
    Academic.

Staub, Ervin (1979). Positive social behavior and morality:
Vol. 2. Socialization and development. New York:
Academic.

Trezza, Alphonse F. (1972). Unselfish cooperation: The
Illinois way. Illinois Libraries, 54, 319-323.

U.S. Government Printing Office (1985), GPO Sales Publications Reference File. Washington, DC: G.P.O.

Walster, Elaine; Walster, G. William; and Berschied, Ellen
(1978). Equity: Theory and research. Boston, MA:
Allyn and Bacon.

Webster's third new international dictionary of the English
language (Unabridged ed.) (1976). Springfield, MA:
G. & C. Merriam.

Weech, Terry L. (1978). The use of government publications: A selected review of the literature. Government
Publications Review, 5, 177-184.

Whyte, William F. (1982). Interviewing in field research.
In Robert G. Burgess (Ed.), Field research: A source-
book and field manual (pp. 111-122). London: George
Allen & Unwin.

Wilke, Henk (1983). Equity: Information and effect dependency. In David M. Messick & Karen S. Cook (Eds.),
Equity theory: Psychological and sociological perspectives (pp. 47-60). New York: Praeger.

Wilson, Pauline (1981). Professionalism under attack! The
Journal of Academic Librarianship, 7, 283-290.

AUTHOR INDEX

179

SUBJECT INDEX